ZEN AND THE ART OF NAVIGATING COLLEGE

MASCOT BOOKS

www.mascotbooks.com

Zen and the Art of Navigating College:
An Inquiry into the True Nature of Education and the Power of Self-Discovery

For more information, please contact:
Mascot Books, an imprint of Amplify Publishing Group
620 Herndon Parkway, Suite 320
Herndon, VA 20170
info@mascotbooks.com

Library of Congress Control Number: 2022923989

CPSIA Code: PRV0323A

ISBN-13: 978-1-63755-508-8

Printed in the United States

Dedication

I dedicate this book to my wife, who has been supportive and understanding unlike anyone I have ever known.

The inspiration for this book came from a lifetime of wandering. Along the way, and largely by serendipity, people came along who helped me enumerate and define my views.

Ruth Woodruff, a writing professor, helped me compose my thoughts. She also helped to expand my range of thought and challenged me to take into consideration other vantage points. She had this uncanny ability to bring up complementary views and perspectives. But most importantly, she provided that much-needed reality check that every writer needs.

I also want to thank Ian Vince, a British scribe who lives for the written word. His matter-of-fact perspective, without emotion or judgment, provided me with confidence that I was putting forth something of value rather than undertaking an exercise in vanity. He gave invaluable guidance and allowed me to test my hypothesis from the perspective of an objective observer.

I also want to thank a college professor who shall go unnamed. After graduating from college, I requested a letter of reference from him to facilitate my entrance to graduate school. Later, I would discover that the letter was far from an endorsement. It turned out to be profoundly critical.

Ironically, his negative reference letter inadvertently aided my acceptance into graduate school. The dean of the accepting graduate school was so jaded by the recurring flow of positive reference letters that he was somewhat enamored by this letter and curious about a student who could engender such heated criticism and admiration. He concluded that I must be harboring some sort of irreverent genius—besides, he was looking to add some salt to the soup.

ZEN *and the* ART *of* NAVIGATING COLLEGE

An Inquiry into the True Nature of Education and the Power of Self-Discovery

PETER KLEIN

Contents

Foreword

UPON REFLECTION, I HAVE BEEN the beneficiary of an excellent education. Having attended a large public high school, I decided to find a small college where I would not get lost in the crowd. In the process, I discovered Goddard College, a small liberal arts school in Vermont with a remarkable 7 to 1 student-to-instructor ratio.

As a student, I was exposed to great instructors. In return, great things were expected from me. At Goddard College, students were expected to take control of their own education and encouraged to take independent study courses in fields of interest, which I believe may have been pioneered at Goddard. But just as importantly, we were guided on how to learn—and in the process encouraged to embrace a lifetime of learning.

I was determined to live a life based on continuous learning; fortune favors those who are prepared. I achieved success in my career, and my affiliation with Goddard College didn't end with my graduation. Decades later, I became vice chairman of its board of trustees.

My fascination with the field of education also led me to

become a board member of the Clay International Secondary School in Makueni County, Kenya, and the chairman of the board of the School for Ethical Education, a grant-making institution supporting ethical and character education in the United States and around the world. Consequentially, my educational perspective runs the gamut from humble student to academic board member and trustee. Needless to say, my life has been a journey.

This book uses a metaphorical journey to describe a student's experience in selecting and attending college. Whenever one refers to a journey, it usually represents adventure, struggle, and change—and that's exactly what I experienced as a student (but unfortunately without the benefit of awareness and perspective offered up in this book).

As Peter Klein smartly points out, Robert Frost's poem, "The Road Not Taken," is a great metaphor because it combines a journey with having to make choices. The poet presents us with a fork in the road. In life, we have to make choices, and in making a choice, we must give something up. This makes decision-making very challenging. Making the truly right decision often requires the benefit of 20/20 hindsight.

The components of proper decision-making are relatively simple but extremely hard to implement. First, one has to gather all relevant information and objectively weigh its pros and cons. Selecting a college and one's major are two of the most consequential decisions we must make, and yet at such an early stage in life, we are extraordinarily ill-prepared. Most of us get it wrong, since 75 percent of college graduates end up in careers having nothing to do with their majors.

We live in world of deceptions, misinformation, illusions, and downright misleading information. And it's all delivered with overwhelming signal noise. How can we make objective decisions in such a world of misinformation? Looking back at my life, even with a quality education, I was ill-prepared to make such significant choices. The challenge is how does one generation explain this to the next generation—or is this something that can only be appreciated through experience?

Ethos, (character) *pathos,* (emotions), and *logos,* (logic) are the three classical modes of persuasion that a person can use to write persuasively. Humbled by life, the author employs logos (reasoning) to convey his insights to the reader, in direct contrast to most academic institutions that expect the student to defer to authority of persons of higher academic standing. It used to be that education was designed to empower the student to make better choices. I'll refer you to the Einstein quote on this book's cover: "Education is not the learning of facts, but the training of the mind to think."

This book provides deep insights into college selection, academic study, and self-discovery. It also alerts the reader to a fundamental understanding of this world—that it is asymmetrical and often unpredictable. In fact, it's sometimes downright confusing, presenting us with dichotomies or worse yet a Faustian bargain. It also is a world that's undergoing changes so profound that they're altering the fundamental fabric of society. Sometimes these changes can lead to the destruction of traditional guardrails, including religion, faith, and personal responsibility.

College offers the chance not only to find and develop a suitable profession but also an opportunity for self-discovery. This book offers the reader greater awareness and perspective that can empower them to better navigate college and achieve far greater outcomes in education and learning. But perhaps more importantly, it helps readers develop an appreciation for the complexity of life and its challenges and offers a toolbox for how to think about and overcome them.

—Peter Donovan,
Chairman of the board
of the School for Ethical Education
and former CEO of Wright Investors' Service

Preface

THERE'S A GAP BETWEEN WHAT students expect and what colleges offer. Ask any graduate. In a recent *Harvard Business Review* study, two-thirds responded that their college or university puts the interests of the institution first, and only 9 percent believed that the students were a priority.[1]

A sizable remainder—just under a quarter—were undecided. This is *not* a ringing endorsement. Moreover, it's one of the most expensive decisions you'll ever make and, at best, is a gamble. Considering the massive investment of time, money, and emotional energy most students throw at their colleges, the experience can potentially turn into an expensive case of buyer's remorse.

It doesn't need to be like this. Armed with the correct information and relevant encouragement, it's possible to navigate your way through college and avoid the pitfalls, U-turns, and dead ends that are so common to the student experience.

Most books about extracting the maximum value from the college experience run along the same lines as a book written by a college professor and a PhD candidate in sociology titled

How College Works.[2] In it they summarize the chronological sequence of predictable challenges faced by students:

- » First, a student must successfully navigate the social world of college.
- » Then they must make academic choices.
- » Then they must establish a broader network composed of student groups that connect them with what's available in the college community.
- » Then, finally, they need to consolidate whatever gains they've made in their college years and move on.

With all due respect, this advice is about as useful as a wax candle without a wick. First of all, it's not very illuminating. Their greater offense, however, is that implicit in the summary is the feeling that all these essential decisions—along with the changes and maturation that the student is simultaneously experiencing—magically come together seamlessly and predictably. The authors fail to recognize a student's anxiety, self-doubt, and strife. All of that stuff is messy, of course. There are no simple, cut-and-dried answers. This is the equivalent of a studio recording engineer concluding a session with the phrase, "Don't worry, we can dub the talent in later."

What sounds so simple, so linear, is far more complex and fraught with unconscious assumptions. In this book, I provide you with unadulterated facts to advance your perspective. What do I mean by perspective? It's typically defined as a technique of depicting volumes and spatial relationships of objects. Rather I am referring to the state of one's ideas, facts known, and their interrelationship. This book attempts to shape a broader point of view from which to sense, categorize, measure, or codify experience.

A broader perspective, designed to help you better navigate your way through the complexities of your college years, would look like this:

- How to take advantage of college facilities you may not know how to access just yet—or may not even be aware of.
- How to look beyond those gifted savants, brainiacs, and dusty academics whose incredible knowledge, specialties, and expertise might inhibit them from taking a wider view of your talents and ambitions.
- How to develop an education that will lead to getting interviews with potential employers.
- How to intentionally develop a meaningful network of colleagues, social friends, and classmates that will stay with you for the rest of your career, offering consequential advantages throughout your life.
- How to strategize the right mix of majors and minors that play to your strengths and develop a demonstrable breadth of knowledge.

Don't be one of the college graduates who experience the educational version of buyer's remorse. Avoid the disappointment caused by the gap between your expectations and reality.

I wrote this book to help fill that gap, but it is up to you to take it and run with it.

If you want to know how to maximize the outcome of your time in college, you'll find the answers in this book. By learning about the pitfalls and problems up-front, you'll factor them into your expectations and plan accordingly. In that way, college will be a rich and amazing experience. You'll be prepared to ensure that it facilitates learning tailored to your strengths, and you'll know how to make the most of the opportunity to meet amazing people and develop lifelong friendships. Then, when you graduate, you'll leave with fewer regrets and more great memories. I wish you luck.

PART I

Choosing the Unexpected Way

WHICH DIRECTION SHOULD YOU TAKE? Knowing you only have one life to live, where will you focus your efforts? How will you decide your direction?

Which path to choose is also the pressing question in the famous poem "The Road Not Taken" by Robert Frost. The poem is written from the perspective of a person facing a difficult decision between two paths:

Two roads diverged in a yellow wood,
And sorry I could not travel both
And be one traveler, long I stood
And looked down one as far as I could
To where it bent in the undergrowth;
Then took the other, as just as fair,
And having perhaps the better claim,
Because it was grassy and wanted wear;
Though as for that the passing there
Had worn them really about the same . . .

As the poet explains, the traveler must choose one direction or the other and regrets that, because he is only one person, he's limited to taking just one of the roads. He knows too that if he chooses one way, he's probably not going to loop back to this juncture. So he encounters both possibility and limitation: every traveler must pick a particular direction in which to walk and, in doing so, relinquish all he might have encountered had he gone the other way.

Given that dilemma, how does the traveler decide which path to walk? What will help him pick the right direction?

Most people face this conundrum of choosing direction as they set out on the journey into adulthood. In this section, we'll address the difficult question of choosing your path.

CHAPTER 1

The Fork in the Road

"It is as impossible to withhold education from the receptive mind as it is impossible to force it upon the unreasoning."

– AGNES REPPLIER

YOU HAVE MADE THE HIGH school grades to qualify and are all set to go to college. Congratulations!

But let's not get ahead of ourselves—you may be heading into higher education, but that is not your ultimate destination. Despite the giddy mix of exhilaration, self-esteem, and optimism you may be feeling right now, college is not an end in and of itself. It's the potentially important next chapter in the story you're creating as you journey through life.

At its best, your college experience can guide you beyond graduation and serve you well for the rest of your life. At its most limited, it can be an expensive distraction from all the things you need to do to find yourself. And find yourself you must, because it's really all about you and your place in the world.

In many ways, the choices you're faced with bear some

resemblance to scenes from the English historical costume drama *Downton Abbey*. After you cut away the lace trimmings and all the bowing and scraping, the first season of *Downton* is all about a choice. Haughty—and very definitely self-important—Lady Mary is faced with a choice between holding out for a marriage of love or jumping into one with a distant cousin who is the new heir apparent to the family's stately home. It's a timeless trope because it's true: love is always pitted against money. In this fictional version of the English aristocracy—spoiler alert—she eventually finds herself in love with the money that will save the country estate. So that's her sorted out—what about you?

Shallow gene pools and arcane inheritance laws aside, you need to find a way to emulate the example; to turn your burning ambition into a life of promise. To reach your potential, you need to uncover the tools that can help you see where your promise lies. The world doesn't make this easy for you and—in many respects—neither does college, but what a higher education does offer is time. Time to explore possibilities. Time to try out subjects and ideas. Time to mold your future to your liking and to your advantage.

And speaking of time, at this exact point in time, you stand at a metaphorical fork in the road; at the head of a journey that overflows with potential—one that should set you off toward not only a worthwhile, rewarding career but also a life with purpose and meaning. You have decisions to make about what you'll study and where you'll study it, and it seems that each of those decisions are pregnant with potential consequences. It's a nerve-racking time.

At the same time, I'm sure that teachers, parents, well-meaning aunts and uncles, older siblings, and family friends have all pointed out the onerous responsibility of balancing your studies with all the other things that college can offer. But I'm not here to just underline what everyone and their dog is telling you. What you really need to know are the techniques and secrets that will significantly enhance the way college works for you. That's where I come in.

Your success starts with the choices of where and what to study, but it also relies on how you learn in the broadest possible sense—not only academically on subjects and curricula, but also on the very subject that all successful people know the best: themselves.

College offers you the opportunity to start a journey in the search for your best self, personally and professionally.

The process of understanding anything starts with understanding yourself and the people around you. Raising your field of vision to gain strategic perspective is vital. You need to strive for improvement and new perspectives, and whenever possible, base your decisions on facts. Let's break that all down into some important considerations before you proceed.

The Difference Between High School and College

The peak of self-discovery and development happens when, as a young man or woman, you achieve a strong enough sense of self that no external disappointment can entirely undermine you. For many college graduates, that begins with the mastery of an advanced education and the development of a knowledge base in one or more disciplines. We all get there through trial and error, hard work, and grit; by failing and learning from our mistakes.

College is the ideal laboratory for self-discovery and building relationships, both of which are just as important for your future as developing subject knowledge and skills.

To do this, you must approach college with a future mindset and leave your high school past behind. In high school, the range of students is as broad as the community, and every student is there because they are compelled to attend. Some students have no plans to attend college and only limited interest in academic achievement. Typically, only a fraction of high school students attend college or even aspire to leave their community.

You may have grown up in the same town, but as you develop, those shared community experiences won't necessarily propel you through your future life. Your high school classmates' aspirations vary widely, but those with ambition will likely have to leave the town they grew up in.

By its very nature, college brings together students who share similar interests and aspirations. College classes typically represent a skewed population in ambition and achievement. If you were exceptional in high school, you may only be average in college.

Plus you're all in the same predicament: trying to acclimate yourself to a whole new world away from your family, community, and friends. Effectively, you are leaving a community defined by geography and joining a community defined by shared interests. There's a reason you all chose to attend this college or university. You have ambition and are willing to invest in yourself and subject yourself to the challenges and stresses that come with academic achievement.

The risk is that college also comes with many temptations, and if you don't prepare to manage these, it can become a place where you lose yourself instead of finding yourself.

Shared Cohort Experience

College offers some unique advantages, including the opportunity to be measured by the same standards by which all college students are assessed. Relative comparison of skills, aptitude, and intelligence allows you to really get to know your fellow students. You'll be given the opportunity to take the full measure of your classmates.

College offers you the opportunity to join a community of men and women of a similar age who share interests and aspirations. It brings together people who ordinarily would never have crossed paths. While some majors do require certain expertise and personality types, other classes can become self-selecting. That offers an opportunity for accidental friendships and fortuitous alliances that could never be replicated in personal life.

You'll meet classmates in your dormitory, in your classes, and in the social and sports activities you join. In the process, you'll likely become acquainted in some form or another with most of the first-year class. On average, the typical freshman class size of a medium-sized college is 1,000 students.

College Offers an Opportunity for Self-Discovery

Deciding on a major is—quite literally—a major challenge. It's a process that presupposes you have undergone some fundamental form of self-discovery and achieved an alignment of aptitude and interest with a career path. Few college entrants have developed such self-awareness, which adds another challenge to overcome.

The problem with college is that if you passively submit yourself to the predetermined college curriculum, it won't—and can't—deliver on your expectations. Rather, you can consider college as a personal retreat that offers you the space to explore. It can offer you an opportunity to develop a clearer vision and better understanding of yourself and your personality and thereby help to eliminate the fog of post-teenage development.

Don't make the mistake that many less-enlightened students do and see your college opportunity as a simple binary choice between extracurricular activities (often in the form of entertainment) or curricular studies. Such students tend to shortchange themselves by selecting the easiest major, choosing classes taught by the least demanding professors, and doing the very minimum they can to "get by." This is sometimes referred to as "majoring in the minors." If you don't take your education seriously, it shouldn't surprise you when it doesn't live up to your expectations. Instead, keep focused on what is important while attending college.

Vast Career Options

Before the modern era, apprenticeships were the norm—you'd learn hands-on skills and expertise from a mature, seasoned worker in your field. The downside was that back then, your job or career was destined. Your future as a carpenter was a designated outcome of the fact that carpentry was what your family had always done.

Today we have more choices, but they come with an inferior

form of learning. Most professions—even today's digitally based jobs—require hands-on training and mentorship.

Today there are virtually no limits to the careers you can choose. But making that choice based on superficial facts will not do. It's easy to misunderstand the attractions of certain careers, simply because so many details of what a job entails are edited out of the description, leaving only the highlights that are easy to admire. The emphasis is on the results, not the labor required to produce them.

It's also easy to be seduced by a romantic or glamorous view of a prospective job, when in fact it entails substantial hardship and tedious labor. Guard against making choices before you've done enough research to weigh the true cost or trade-off of each career you're considering. And rise above the temptation to pursue occupations that pay well and look good on the surface but require the sacrifice of your ambition.

Finding Direction

A fortunate few can identify their passion and corresponding skill sets at an early age. We've all witnessed classmates who seem to exemplify such talent and skill, secure in their choice of major. They're passionate about their field and see no need to consider any other discipline.

For those of us who may see ourselves as less talented, we engage less and may even be bored. Boredom is a signal that we're failing to interact with the world. We've lost our way and aren't being as effective as we were meant to be. Like other negative emotions, such as anger and sadness, it's possible that boredom evolved to motivate us. What we're really searching for is to be cognitively engaged. We're demonstrating our need to use our mental resources for something that's meaningful to us.

Let's consider a few stories of people who attempted to figure out what was essential for them when they were at the same age as modern-day college entrants.

The first is Henry David Thoreau (1817–1862) who was an impromptu philosopher and writer known for his attacks on institutions and his respect for nature and simple living. Thoreau is most famous for his book *Walden,* which documents his experiences living alone on Walden Pond in Massachusetts for more than two years.

Thoreau attended Harvard University, which he did not particularly like. It turns out he was not particularly likable. One classmate recalled his "look of smug satisfaction," like a man "preparing to hold his future views with great setness and personal appreciation of their importance."

After graduating, he held a variety of jobs but displayed no commitment to a career. He worked as a schoolteacher, then helped run a school with his older brother, John. When John died of tetanus, Thoreau's experiments in the practice of teaching ended, as well.

Afterward, he built a cabin on Walden Pond where he lived for two years. It then took him nearly 10 years to complete the book about his experience.

The real Thoreau was self-obsessed, narcissistic, fanatical about self-control, and adamant that he required nothing beyond himself to understand and thrive in the world. Alternatively, he was an eloquent spokesperson and a prescient voice for the preservation of wild places. But *Walden* is less a cornerstone work of environmental literature than a sort of cabin isolation fantasy. Thoreau's nearest neighbor lived only a mile away. The book was really about the idea of a rustic life divorced from reality—an escape from the entanglements and responsibilities of living among other people.

Thoreau went to Walden Pond to learn to survive with only the essentials. He wanted to try subsistence living—a condition attractive chiefly to those not obliged to endure it. It appealed to Thoreau because he "wanted to live deep and suck out all the marrow of life, to live so sturdily and Spartan-like as to put to rout all that was not life."

Walden was a referendum on possessions and materialism. Thoreau eschewed these because he believed they got in the way of finding oneself. However, shunning material possessions and failing to maintain a life of wellness and good nutrition meant that he came down with tuberculosis, a disease for which—in Thoreau's time—there was no cure.

Throughout his life, Thoreau emphasized the importance of individuality and self-reliance. However, on and off he worked as a land surveyor and in the family pencil factory. He never married. He died at just 44 years old in his mother's home with essentially no belongings.[3]

Very Few Know Early

The other extreme is the person who seems to know their vocation almost from birth. Such was the case of Albert Einstein. His family operated an electrical generator manufacturing company. One of his first scientific essays dealt with the effect of magnetism on the hypothetical "ether." It was written when he was 16, apparently as part of his first attempt to gain admission to the Federal Institute of Technology in Zurich—which was unsuccessful.

It was the relationship of electricity and magnetism to light waves, as defined a decade earlier by James Clerk Maxwell, which helped put Einstein on the road toward his first theory of relativity. As Einstein wrote later, Maxwell's theory was "the most fascinating subject at the time that I was a student." But as former professor of physics at Boston University and Einstein scholar, Dr. John Stachel, pointed out recently, the Einstein electrical manufacturing enterprise failed, first in Munich and then in Italy, where the Einstein family moved after the first business was unsuccessful. Their son, Albert, was excelling in his classes at the Luitpold Gymnasium in Munich, but he hated it there and soon followed the family to Italy.

The scope of the Einstein family's—including his father, Hermann, and his more scientifically-minded Uncle Jakob—electrical manufacturing activity was more significant than first understood by historians. It now appears that the Einstein enterprise was internationally recognized and considerably more innovative than previously suspected. Technical journals in Britain, France, Italy, and Germany reveal that one of its devices, an electric meter, was patented in the United States and that the Einstein company built the central power station for a Munich suburb.[4]

Another testament to Einstein's intelligence comes from Dr. Max Talmey who, as a medical student in Munich, knew the young Einstein when he was just 10 years old. His "exceptional intelligence," Talmey wrote in his 1932 book, *The Relativity Theory Simplified and the Formative Period of Its Inventor*, enabled him to discuss with a college graduate "subjects far beyond the comprehension" of such a young child. Talmey gave him two books on physics, one of which was entitled *Force and Matter*, as though anticipating Einstein's famous definition of the relationship between mass and energy.[5]

Figuring It Out Serendipitously

Albert Einstein represents a very small minority of people who seem to know their direction in life from an early age. Most of us figure it out as we go through life and often find our way by trial and error.

Some people seem to discover their path serendipitously, just by happening to come across something that clicks into place for them. That's how Carl Jung figured out what he wanted to pursue as a career.

Jung, the noted turn-of-the-century Swiss psychiatrist, contributed significantly to mankind's knowledge of the human condition. Looking at the arc of Jung's life, you might assume that he had it easy and intuitively knew at an early age that he had a passion for psychiatry.

But in truth, Jung had a volatile, uncertain childhood. His mother suffered from psychological problems that led to a stint in a mental institution, and his father was barely able to eke out a living. Jung was a solitary and introverted child. His mother's psychological issues caused the young Jung considerable consternation. During his early childhood, he didn't have the best relationship with his parents. He considered his mother to be a good mother, but he felt that her true personality was always hidden from him.

As Jung grew older, he was drawn to various sciences, as well as the history of religion, making the selection of a career quite difficult. However, he finally decided on medicine, following the example of his grandfather, a noted physician. Jung studied at the University of Basel (1895–1900) and received his medical degree from the University of Zurich in 1902.

Throughout medical school, he was uncertain of which specialty he would enter. By serendipity, while studying for his final exam, he came across a textbook on psychiatry. As he thumbed through the pages, he came upon the words "maladjusted personalities." According to interviews he gave, it was at that very instant that he knew he would be specializing in psychiatry. Everything just clicked into place for him.

He focused his studies and ultimately his practice on psychiatry, even at the expense of an invitation to join one of his professors in practice at a leading Zurich medical center. This was a radical departure for someone raised in a Swiss German community that emphasized the legitimacy of perfectionism, frowned upon radical views, and abhorred any kind of flaws in judgment or behavior.

Furthermore, as a pre-med student, his professors were very critical of his writing skills and were concerned about his ability to complete his dissertation. Nonetheless, he prevailed and graduated. Not long after beginning his practice, Jung published his first book, *Studies in Word Association*, which was ultimately reviewed by Dr. Sigmund Freud.[6]

Jung went on to be a fearless writer and published many books. His largely intuitive findings about human psychology and behavior have had a profound impact—not just on psychology but in the business world and society at large.

Deciding on Your Major

Choosing a major is one of the most important milestones in your college experience, and it's a decision that will influence your career trajectory—for better or worse. Whatever you choose to do for a living will probably govern 70 percent of your life ahead. Thus, it helps if your career choice is fundamentally in sync with who you are! When your occupation matches your personality type, it has a substantial impact on your job satisfaction.

In the first two years of college, all students must take a certain number of required general courses before they commit to a major. This gives you time to discover yourself and your true personality traits. Why don't colleges use that time to aid students in self-understanding and self-discovery? Most colleges don't provide any assistance at all. You're on your own.

Additionally, the process of self-discovery isn't linear, and it can take an unpredictable amount of time. It's a complex process laced with uncertainty. Ideally, schools would assist students in aligning their aptitude and interests with their ideal career path. Rather than doing so, most colleges simply emphasize graduating on time.

There's really nothing more critical to your education than learning who you really are, so you must prioritize understanding who you are and take this task upon yourself—not just in college, but as you go forward in life. As humans, we constantly grow and evolve. Staying in touch with who you are at your very core can be difficult in such a fast-paced world. When you lose touch with who you are, you risk losing perspective. Taking time for self-discovery can help you get back in touch and allow you to stay focused on what's most important in your life.

Knowing yourself gives you the kind of confidence that

makes you less vulnerable to the judgment of others. It allows you to maintain perspective, even when being criticized. It helps you stand up for yourself when under attack and helps you better manage disputes by enabling you to remain rational and composed.

Self-Knowledge 101

Your personality and values will always govern what you enjoy doing. These aspects of yourself must be considered in the evaluation process to determine a suitable career. A good match means you're more likely to be successful and will enjoy going to work.

Personality quizzes can be a great way to remind yourself of your strengths, which can boost confidence and help generate pride. Reading through your personality test results can help you marshal the strengths you possess. After all, they summarize everything that makes you unique while highlighting your innate talents.

Personality tests can also help you make better career choices. Career-focused assessments help you discover what type of company culture is the best fit for your personality type, and they can help you discover career strengths and weaknesses. Armed with this kind of information, you can learn how to thrive in your career and find a job that suits you.

Interestingly, it was Jung's personality theory that contributed significantly to a widely used personality test, the Myers-Briggs Type Indicator. From his years of psychoanalysis of patients, Jung was able to identify certain personality trait patterns. The first overarching category he defined was extroverts versus introverts. In 1921, Jung published the book *Psychological Types*, where he laid out his theory of personality. He believed that each person has a psychological type. He wrote, "what appears to be random behavior is actually the result of differences in the way people prefer to use their mental capacities."[7]

Some people, he observed, mainly take in information—which he labeled perceiving—while others mainly organize it and draw conclusions—which he called judging. He also believed that there are four psychological functions. Thinking asks the question, "What does it mean?" This involves making judgments and decisions. Feeling asks the question, "What value does this have?" Judging, for instance, may be determining right versus wrong. Sensation asks, "What exactly am I experiencing?" This involves how we perceive the world and gather information using our different senses. Intuition asks, "What might happen; what is possible?" This refers to how perception relates to things like goals and past experiences.

Inspired by Jung's work, Isabel Myers and her mother Katharine Cook Briggs created the *Myers-Briggs Type Indicator*. They developed the personality measure in the 1940s, which consists of 16 personality types.[8]

I recently reconnected with an old college classmate. After many phone calls exchanging stories and sharing experiences and accomplishments about the intervening decades, I asked him if he'd ever taken a personality test. He didn't know what it was. I was curious because he had accomplished something quite difficult. He had gone from graduating at the top of his class as a chemistry major to ultimately becoming a journalist and newsletter editor. Later, I discovered that he had attended college on a full scholarship and had qualified as a Merit Scholar.

After graduation, he worked for two years as a research chemist at Xerox, a dream job for someone fresh out of college. But he didn't feel fulfilled. He became restless and left. He spent several years hitchhiking and taking odd jobs, including such roles as a zoo handler in Florida and a grounds person at a gated community—this was not a fit, and he was fired. He spent several years wandering in the wilderness, so to speak. He had embarked on this journey to discover himself and his interests.

Somehow, my friend drifted into journalism—with stints as a freelance reporter and columnist—which would ultimately become his chosen career. What's amazing is that he had successfully transitioned from being a quantitative scientist to becoming a writer, a man of letters, a qualitative scrivener.

I can tell you from experience that science majors are typically not known for their writing ability. They tend to be highly quantitative people who can visualize and dissect scientific theory and hypothesize its applications. As a rule, quantitative people are very different from qualitative people. They tend to be more methodical, introverted, and process-oriented. They're generally not known for their people skills. Scientific research requires considerable discipline, rigorous methodology, and unrelenting consistency. I'd always assumed that he had those personality traits.

Effectively, he had to overcome substantial barriers in his migration—out-of-phase skill sets, left versus right brain abilities, extrovert versus introvert personality traits—while developing highly advanced writing and communication skills. Crossing such perceived barriers without the aid and confidence offered by clinical aptitude testing is amazing.

Again, a school of higher learning should assist students in aligning their aptitude and interests with their ideal career path. If colleges took more of an interest in linking each student's aptitude with his or her career path, it would more likely result in students being more thoughtful as they select a major. And it would greatly improve their overall satisfaction with their college experience. Most colleges, however, make little to no effort to assist their students—and almost 50 percent of graduating students regret their choice of major.

Academic Advisors

Most college students don't have their futures planned out from start to finish, and that's okay—that's why you're assigned an academic advisor. These individuals are trained to help you map out your college career and guide you through the process of achieving your goals. Sure, you can probably do it all on your own, but why would you want to if you don't have to? You have access to someone who knows how to get you from point A to point B, effectively and efficiently. Make the most of that service.

Career Centers

Sometimes it's helpful to put together a fantasized résumé that you think you will need to land your first job. One of those elements is having work experience that complements your academic credentials. Identifying work that you can do during the summer or assistance you can provide to a professor can serve as the basis for building an impressive résumé.

The college guidance center can alert you to internships that are available to those who take the initiative. Contacting successful alumni can also lead to temporary job opportunities. When garnering these jobs or internship opportunities, work with the campus career center to develop materials that can be used in interviews.

Creating your first résumé and cover letter can be daunting, but with the proper help and guidance from the career center, you can ensure yours attracts the proper attention. The staff can also aid you in preparing any materials you may need for your job or internship search. Building a relationship with the staff at the career center can ultimately aid you in landing your first important job.

Counseling

Most colleges are aware that students get overwhelmed at times. That's why many offer free counseling sessions for students—to help you find healthy ways to cope with feeling over-stressed, depressed, or anxious. Your school wants you to remain healthy, both mentally and physically, so don't hesitate to take advantage of this resource as needed.

But there is another use for these support services, and that's for the purposes of self-discovery. Identifying your innate traits and understanding how they can impact your behavior and career path success will allow you to lead a better life with greater opportunities for happiness. Unless you take the initiative towards self-discovery, you are likely to get battered by life.

In subsequent chapters, we'll examine another important way to start figuring out who you are (or at least start the process), what do you enjoy studying, and how to position yourself to succeed in college and beyond. Instead of narrowing your focus, it involves broadening your view and sampling as wide a range of subjects as possible.

CHAPTER 2

Wander the Amazing Maze

"The things taught in schools and colleges are not an education but the means of an education."

– RALPH WALDO EMERSON

The Illusion of the Straight Path and Simple Symmetry

If the only thing standing between you and your life's ambition is a college degree, believe me, you are blessed. Few things in life are that simple or straightforward. You wouldn't be the first to believe in the transformative power of a piece of paper or to regard it as a form of driver's license for your life. But think about that metaphor for a moment. When you pass your driver's test, you're nowhere near to being an expert driver; it takes years of practice, a few hopefully-not-too-serious mistakes, and a personality more or less suited to piloting a two-ton steel machine around the highway. It's not all about the exam.

Nevertheless, most students fresh out of high school believe that getting a college degree is all that stands between them and their life's ambition. In our youth, we see the world in symmetrical terms based on a simple linear progression. We compose a vision for our life story based on the idea of a straight path and our simple, symmetrical view. It is a well-trodden path set before us by so many others.

We can see repeating motifs in glorified ambitions. Most of these dreams are variations on the classic "rags to riches" story, or they involve writing the great novel or achieving some scientific or technological breakthrough.

Up until the start of college, your life has been shaped and sheltered by your family and a highly choreographed education system. That education system is progressive by nature, moving from one grade to the next, and it remains linear if you excel at—or at least meet—the minimum academic standards set. Consequently, you see life as a linear progression, marked by certain achievements and with thresholds or rites of passage that are achieved by age, academic performance, or the simple act of completion.

Just as we have experienced education in progressive and linear terms, we also tend to project that same kind of thinking in our careers. We see ourselves moving from promotion to promotion, putting in the time, and believing that the risk of not performing adequately and losing a job is something that happens to others. To paraphrase an old song by The Carpenters, in our youth we tend to "ask perfection of a quite imperfect world."

The problem with that view is that it doesn't square with real life. The idea that college offers you the opportunity to develop a clearer vision and better understanding of yourself and your personal attributes is real. But it will require you to take control of your course load. At the same time, your mind is undergoing dramatic changes as part of a process of post-adolescent brain development.

A fascinating and valuable way to approach this is to allow yourself to wander and sample some of the amazing maze of opportunities that college presents. Recognize that you're stepping into a maze with lots of twists and turns; one that allows you to test out multiple paths, knowing full well that not every direction will be the right one for you. It's fine to hit a dead end now and then—in fact, you can expect that to happen as you find your way by trial and error. The idea is to keep an open mind and stick to your commitment to learning. Even in those instances where you come up against a wall, you'll gain valuable insights into who you are and where you should be headed. So explore your options, figure out what works for you and what doesn't, and develop stick-to-it-iveness and a sense of curiosity that will keep you motivated along the way.

Animal Instincts, Animal Behavior

Life is asymmetrical and nonlinear; it's messy, complicated, sometimes chaotic, and intermingled with catastrophe. You will experience rejection, failure, and loss. You will witness many transitions and disruptions to your hopes and dreams.

Human nature is complicated; but when we are young, we see only the superficial and predictable. Many of the decisions we're asked to make appear to be simply binary in nature, but some will be laced with potential pitfalls, entanglements, and difficulty. So often we discover unanticipated consequences to our actions. Life can and does impose its will, and we'll be faced with significant decisions that will have profound consequences.

We think of ourselves as being above animals, and yet we share many similarities, including a number of instinctive behaviors we developed to survive. We're hard-wired to avoid loss when comfortable but scramble madly when catastrophe strikes. Although humanity has progressed through hundreds of millennia, we're still bridled by these instinctive behaviors and must accept the fact that we share some instincts with the rest of the animal kingdom. Think of how the fear of snakes is inherent in us, for example. Our ability to recognize warning signals, and our instinctive fight-or-flight response is just as present in us as it is in the animal kingdom.

What separates humans from animals is an oversized, complex brain and hands built for manipulation. It's what makes us capable of understanding the workings of the universe, microbiology, and our own innate human behavior. Nevertheless, we've been hard-wired with a specific set of traits that have served us in the past but may lead to problems today.

Consequently, we need to be aware and informed of nature's way. For example, nature abhors a straight line. You can look virtually everywhere in nature without finding one. It's only when you look at *inorganic* molecules at either the microscopic level or as crystals that you will see straight line geometric patterns. In organic life, there are no straight lines, and nothing in nature is 100 percent. Animals and humans alike are not 100 percent heterosexual; homosexual behavior is evident in the animal kingdom. DNA differences mean that medical treatments are not 100 percent effective, nor are vaccines. Nature is not concerned about perfection or exact replication; it's more concerned with sustainability while testing survival.

Nature dictates, in part, the tune by which we live. Natural sciences and nature share certain traits. One of the most common misconceptions concerns so-called "scientific proof." Contrary to popular belief, there is no such thing as a scientific proof in natural sciences. Proofs exist only in mathematics and logic. Mathematics and logic are both closed, self-contained systems of propositions, whereas science is empirical and deals with nature as it exists. The primary criterion and standard of evaluation of scientific theory is evidence, not proof. All else being equal (such as internal logical consistency and parsimony), scientists prefer theories for which there is more and better evidence to theories for which there is less and worse evidence.

Proofs have two features that do not exist in science: they are final, and they are binary. Once a theorem is proven, it will forever be true and nothing in the future will threaten its status. Apart from the discovery of an error, a proven theorem will forever and always be a proven theorem.

Encountering an Imperfect World

I was working on a laboratory project in college, or at least I was going through the motions, when I had my first rude encounter as a young adult with the imperfection of how things really work. I was nursing a low-grade infection—not sick enough to be in bed, but not well enough to tackle my course load and student obligations. The lab assignment involved a chemical reaction producing a specific hydrocarbon molecule. It was a relatively common reaction and, as it so happened, a bottle of the molecule was stored in the chemistry lab annex. I had planned to sneak into the lab over the weekend to complete the reaction. But I took a small amount of the final product from the lab to buy time in the event I was challenged for not completing my assignment during the reserved lab time.

Nothing in nature is pure in its chemistry. Rather, it's like the breakfast cereal that proclaims "made with 100 percent whole wheat," yet which also shows a caveat on the side of the box warning "this product may contain nuts." Nothing is 100 percent. This applies to chemical reactions; there are always impurities, and it takes a lot of work to remove them, including distillation, filtration through activated carbon, and so on. This became an issue in my lab assignment. My instructor, a senior student, wanted to see what I had produced, and he was surprised at its purity and clarity. I mumbled about distilling it and filtering the solution through activated carbon to provide some plausible deniability. He knew what I had done, but fortunately for me, he chose not to pursue the matter. Any seasoned science student knows that there is no such thing as 100 percent in the natural sciences. In a way, this mutually shared knowledge was just another example of how we had progressed from our adolescent innocence into the real world of how things actually work.

Later, in graduate school, I learned another important lesson; most research is esoteric and of little consequence. In our youth, we seek perfection in a quite imperfect world. We're a product of nature, and no matter how far above nature we may view ourselves to be, it has a tendency to cast a shadow across our best laid plans.

Most of us may well find ourselves disappointed when we

realize the basic imperfection of reality, and we may even cringe about our pointless existence. Often we move from one scene to the next, without purpose. We wander from high school to college, from college to our first job. Then we're dying to get married, then to have children. Next, we're dying to get our kids out of the house. Then we're dying to retire, only to find out that we're really just dying—never having known why we were alive in the first place.

The reality is that we don't have any real appreciation for the risks and consequences in life. One of those risks is that our lives become something else: an assembly of habits, objects, and impulses, and not even a story at all.

The Disparity Between the Promise of College and Jobs Realized

In several studies, reviewing the outcome of some two million graduating students in America, only 27 percent of graduates had a job related to their major. The vast majority of American college graduates can't find work in jobs directly relevant to their degrees. To make matters worse, only 62 percent of post-collegiate young people have a job that requires a college degree.[9]

A common refrain seems to run along the lines of: "My degree didn't really come in handy for my new job, but college itself was still useful." Students need to keep perspective on what's truly important. It's hard to understand why a college education seems to be one of the few things in life that we put so much time and money into while demanding so little in return. Would you go to a car dealership, pay for an expensive new sports car, and drive away in an old, beat-up minivan? When education is so valuable, doesn't it make sense to demand the maximum value for our tuition dollars?

In my own experience, the education provided by my college was incredibly disappointing and lacking in real-world applications. I was able to compensate to some degree by taking the initiative to extract more from my time there. I nearly doubled my course load, studying subjects in a variety of disciplines—some of which were completely unrelated to my science major.

Taking Yourself Seriously

If you passively submit yourself to a typical college curriculum, it won't and can't deliver on your expectations. If you have a plan, college can offer the opportunity to develop a clearer vision and better understanding of yourself and your personal attributes. At the same time, your mind is undergoing dramatic changes resulting in a clearing of the fog of post-teenage development that may have clouded your judgment and focus. For some, that cloud lingers on, and they may be prone to see college attendance as a simple binary choice between extracurricular activities or curricular studies. Either way, students end up shortchanging themselves.

Costs of Shortcuts

There are hidden costs to taking shortcuts in college. Here's a story to illustrate this.[10]

One night, four college students were out partying, rather than studying for a test the next day. In the morning, they hatched a plan. They spread grease and dirt on themselves and went to the dean. They told him they'd gone out to a wedding and on their way back, a tire burst on their car, and they had to push the car all the way back late into the night. They told the dean that they were in no condition to take the test. The dean thought for a minute and allowed them to take a re-test in three days. They thanked him and said they would be ready by that time.

On the third day, they appeared before the dean. The dean said that as this was a special test, he would require certain conditions: all four were required to sit in separate classrooms to take the exam. They all agreed as they had prepared well in the last three days. The test consisted of only two questions for a total of 100 points:

1. What is your name? ____________________
2. Which tire burst? ____________________

The lesson is to be careful in conspiring to game the system. These students were focused on partying and entertainment, rather than academic pursuit, and they failed to take personal responsibility for their actions. The dean, a veteran of many student campaigns, set up a trap to unravel their story. He created a teachable moment by unmasking their conspiracy and forcing them to confess and acknowledge their deception and take responsibility for their dishonesty.

The dean's exposure to juvenile behavior taught him that adolescents are highly motivated by pleasure and immediate gratification, regardless of consequences. He knew teenagers engage in risky behavior because they're still developing the brain function to weigh the long-term consequences of their decisions.

It's not that teenagers are intentionally irresponsible or unwise. Science tells us they lack the brain anatomy to make the connections necessary to think, "This may end poorly for me or negatively affect my future." They don't have the mechanisms in place yet to tap the brakes when something pleasurable comes up.

The dean's test was designed to call the students' attention to their mockery of the institution. Cornered, they would have to confess and face the consequences of their action. The dean knew that by holding them accountable and meting out some form of punishment, the exercise would get them to reflect and modify their behavior and possibly accelerate the maturing process.

The other lesson is that you can't take a shallow dive into gaining an education. You must prepare for several transitions, including selecting a suitable major, graduating, finding a job, developing a career, and stepping into the responsibility of adulthood. These students viewed their college degree as simply a stepping stone to the next phase of their lives, thinking that the substance of their education didn't matter.

Sample Some Minors

Being engaged in your college experience is a necessary first step for learning. Sitting passively in class, not really absorbing the material and only half-heartedly attempting to study, is a recipe for disappointment. The college experience requires participating in class and building a road map to extract the most out of your college experience and education. The process of becoming educated requires the absorption of the material, the processing and dissection of that information, comprehension, and cataloging it in your brain. This can only be accomplished through engagement. As a Chinese proverb states, "Tell me and I'll forget; show me and I may remember; involve me and I'll understand."

A broad background and understanding enhances our power to observe and comprehend, and it ultimately leads to better decision-making. This makes it important to focus on subjects and practices that we are passionate about, but not at the expense of developing a greater awareness about other important subjects. Although biologically we have great binocular vision, we are often blinded by our inability to process and comprehend what we see. We also have binaural hearing which allows our ears to sense the direction of sounds, but it's up to the brain to interpret those sounds. Consequently, a stream of words that include specialized vocabulary will often be ignored since they don't register with our brain.

College offers you the opportunity to learn more, think deeper, be tested, and find your passion. College tuition is the price of exposure to a wide array of subjects. You can gain exposure to subjects in which you already have some familiarity, or you can pursue subjects that you have avoided in the past or of which you were completely unaware. College coursework will challenge you—you'll be going into much more depth and detail—but perhaps its most important intellectual benefit is that it will enable you to find your passion. When you engage in multiple disciplines, the opportunity to explore a range of interests may lead you to passions that you never knew you had.

It's an exploratory time for you if you take advantage of these opportunities. In the words of Andrew Delbanco, Columbia University professor, "Take stock of [your] talents and passions and begin to sort [your life] in a way that is true to [yourself] and responsible to others."[11] Perhaps you already know what you want to do with your life, but for most students, college provides the opportunity to explore all your options and find the things that you care about most. College can help you find your purpose, but you must take the initiative.

You'll find that, even in your freshman year, an overwhelming quantity of information is being flung at you, along with homework and writing assignments. By the third year, your load of general courses has largely been completed, leaving you free to focus on your major. I decided to take the full amount of credit hours included in my tuition payment each semester. Normally, students try to reduce their course load to focus on achieving better grades in their major, while paying the same amount in tuition. You can focus on your grades while still making the most of your tuition by opting to take elective courses on a pass-fail basis.

Essential Minors

There are four disciplines involved in today's modern society for comprehension and understanding to occur: human behavior/psychology; economics/commerce; science, including medicine; and geopolitical history. Of these, there are two essential disciplines that we all should have exposure to since they are so pervasive in everyday life—commerce and human psychology. It's important to be exposed to other disciplines, even if they may conflict with your own passions.

The writer F. Scott Fitzgerald, famously wrote: "The test of a first-rate intelligence is the ability to hold two opposing ideas in mind at the same time and still retain the ability to function. One should, for example, be able to see that things are hopeless and yet be determined to make them otherwise."

Commerce is part of our everyday life. Beginning at the local coffee shop, we conduct a series of daily transactions. Small businesses rely on our expenditures. We live in a capitalist society under a social order in which private property rights and the free market serve as the basis of trade, distribution of goods, and development. That's how our world works. The second influencing factor is understanding that capitalism is based on creating value.

If you are living in a capitalist society, you need to have a basic understanding of how business and the economy work. This involves gaining exposure to economics, business practices, management, and capital markets and investment.

For whatever reason, we have always had a love-hate relationship with business and finance. Instead, think of it this way: capitalism is the only system where you can *choose* your place. Effectively, an essential difference between capitalism and every other system is one of opportunity. It offers the opportunity for someone born into poverty to gain wealth, or it allows someone born into wealth to deplete it. The Chinese have a saying: "From rice paddy to rice paddy in three generations or less." The Dutch have a similar saying: "From clogs to clogs in three generations or less." In China, working in a rice paddy is the lowest of economic achievement, while a Dutch person wearing clogs indicates they can't afford leather shoes. The point is the same: it takes opportunity and effort to avoid falling into generational work ruts.

Commerce allows for the exchange of a product or service

in return for more value. In a successful transaction, everyone gets wealthier because they have done something that increases the current value of the product or service in some way. Take, for example, a farmer who buys $500 of seed. In a closed universe, this is a zero-sum transaction. The trade is done, and that's the end of the transaction. In the real world, though, this is potentially a positive-sum transaction. The farmer will plant these seeds and harvest the grain to sell for a profit and generate wealth. The consumer buys the products made from the grain, and each party gets something that has more value to them.[12]

However, capitalism doesn't *ensure* that every participant achieves gains. The capital markets demand efficiency in order to meet consumers' needs at a competitive price. Some business operators will miscalculate the market and suffer financially. The marketplace plays no favorites. In almost all trades, deals, and financial contracts, the world is far bigger than a zero-sum game. Almost nothing happens in a closed universe.

A good metaphor for capitalism is the floor of the jungle. Underneath the jungle canopy is a constant recycling of organic vegetation and animal life. New growth emerges only to decay and decompose, which then provides nourishment for the next emerging vegetation. Capitalism is much the same. New businesses form all the time, but most either fail or don't grow beyond their initial purpose. Only a few grow into substantial companies. From there, they might reach the mature phase and then decline as they are replaced by more efficient businesses—or in some cases, undermined by the advent of disruptive technology.

Life at the bottom of the jungle floor is subject to considerable recycling and change. This also takes place in commerce. But economists give it a nice spin; they call it "creative disruption."

Every small business that fails may well ruin someone's life, financially. There are fiscal consequences. As in nature, the marketplace is very demanding and in a constant state of change subjected to creative disruption. Sometimes it's very gradual and almost imperceptible. Other times, it's sudden and disruptive.[13]

Today, businesspeople are often trained to dispense with emotions in favor of rational analysis and are urged to make choices using logical devices such as decision trees and spreadsheets. But evolutionary psychology suggests that emotions can never fully be suppressed. That's why even the most sensible employees struggle to accept feedback in the constructive vein in which it's generally given. Because of the primacy of emotions, people hear the bad news first and loudest.

The evolving human mind, according to evolutionary psychologists, is hard-wired in ways that govern human behavior to this day. It sheds light on why people act in ways that don't appear to be beneficial to themselves or to their careers. In some situations, they do the unthinkable. They scream at their bosses or perform other acts of aggression. Instead of acting rationally, they flame out in a panic to survive. For some of us, it's easy to descend into a spiral of self-pity and outrage when things don't go as planned. That's why we must practice rising above our instincts, so we can avoid these embarrassments and improve our lives for the better.

"Playing well with others" is essential to advancing one's career, but it often requires the development of new skills. Collaborators must adapt to others' ways of working, cede the spotlight to the team rather than hogging it, and speak up when they disagree with colleagues—even when they're afraid of angering others or looking stupid. These skills often go against our basic instincts, but we must practice and develop them to succeed in the world today.

Developing a Growth Mindset

The Growth Mindset is a concept developed by Stanford Professor of Psychology Dr. Carol Dweck in her 2006 book, *Mindset: Changing the Way You Think to Fulfill Your Potential.*[14] In *Mindset,* Dweck explains that it's not just our abilities and talents that bring success but also whether we approach them with a fixed or growth mindset. People with a fixed mindset believe in an innate fixed state of ability for themselves. They avoid things they have failed at before and tend to give up easily when challenged by a problem or task. Those with a growth mindset believe that they can develop abilities and skills through dedication and practice. In life, it's possible to alternate between the two states, and it's also possible to cultivate your growth mindset to use it to its best effect. Better still, the growth mindset is something of a self-fulfilling prophecy—it's been shown that merely engaging in a growth mindset will exercise the mind in such a way that it starts to make better connections. During college, you have an unrivalled opportunity to work on your mind's growth in a fundamental way.

If you can exploit your college experience to gain exposure to other disciplines, you can develop an understanding of a wide array of subjects along with their lexicons. Each one has its own vocabulary, which can serve as a barrier to outsiders. In the digital age, each profession has garnered mountains of information, with its own unique nomenclature and idioms. To have any chance of developing an understanding of other disciplines, one must have a fundamental understanding of that discipline's terminology.

Inference can be defined as the process of forming a conclusion based on available evidence plus previous knowledge and experience. It's a chance to empower yourself and achieve an opportunity for lifelong learning through what I call "inference reading," but it can only be achieved by developing an understanding of the lexicons of a broad array of subjects. I use search services to collect articles on a range of topics that I read daily. This helps me stay up-to-date and build on my basis of understanding in several subjects.

Our brains are elaborately wired for categorization of facts. Establishing a lifelong pursuit of inference reading and learning can develop a growth mindset. Living in a fast-changing, technology-driven society requires us to keep up with ever-changing technology and its impact on society. This can only be done by cultivating a habit of inference reading.

When you have a growth mindset, you'll perceive challenges as learning opportunities and push through them. Science shows that pushing through difficulty literally helps to grow the brain. It's like exercising a muscle—you have to use it and break it down in order to build it back up. It's all about effort and learning, not about avoiding the risk of making mistakes.

Getting Gritty

Education, exposure to a range of disciplines, and experience can enhance our ability to transform a hopeless situation into a controlled and constructive rebound in which we emerge stronger from the ordeal. Composure and assurance in oneself depend upon our ability to take destructive events and adversity and turn them into positive learning experiences. Getting fired could be a godsend if it leads to self-examination and improvement. In each person's life, the chances of only good things happening are extremely slim. The likelihood that our desires will always be fulfilled is minute. It's more likely that we will be repeatedly disappointed and experience frequent hits to our self-esteem. This is why we must develop the courage, resilience, perseverance, and coping skills to counter these assaults to our confidence.

It's also worth remembering that a career that goes from one success or promotion to another cannot teach you as much about yourself as a patch of adversity. It might be comfortable to have things go your way, but there's a lot of fun and excitement in turning your fortunes around, and there's a qualitative difference to how you feel about your triumphs when they are harder won. If you seek to find yourself in your work, you'll be grateful for the opportunity to prove that you can overcome difficulty and still achieve great things. Along the way, you should remember that the journey itself is the meaning of your life—not the destination.

Everyone has to undergo personal struggle to find themselves and navigate life, and avoiding the challenge will not make life easier. Jung said it best: "There is no coming to consciousness without pain. People will do anything, no matter how absurd, to avoid facing their own inner self. One does not become enlightened by imagining figures of light, but by making the darkness conscious."

Dealing positively with struggle and adversity is adopting Dweck's growth mindset under special circumstances and with a bigger stake in play, because having a fixed mindset in such a predicament is potentially catastrophic.

Conduct More Accurate Simulations

Broadening one's perspective and developing an understanding of many disciplines advances one's comprehension, and ability to categorize and codify experience. It can lead to better problem-solving abilities. It can empower a person to live life under a greater degree of control rather than constantly live in fear. Everything we do in life, we do twice. First, we run a simulation in our mind, then we physically perform the procedure or task. Professional golfers use visualization before striking the ball; they play out and imagine their golf shot first, which enhances their ability to make the play. The more we know about other disciplines, the more variables we can entertain, and the more accurately our simulation will run. Our mental preparation is only as good as the interdisciplinary knowledge we possess and our ability to identify all the variables.

Stephen R. Covey, in *The 7 Habits of Highly Effective People*, refers to this concept: "All things are created twice."[15] Covey suggests that there's a mental creation first, followed by a physical creation. "Take the construction of a home, for example. You create it in every detail before you ever hammer the first nail into place.... Then you reduce it to a blueprint and develop construction plans. You must make sure that the blueprint, the first creation, is really what you want, that you've thought everything through. Then you put it into bricks and mortar. Through imagination, we can visualize the uncreated worlds of potential that lie within us."

The power of visualization is that anything you can imagine you can make real—the only constraints being the natural laws of the universe. This is a useful exercise for imagining many possible outcomes. You test and hone the details in your mind, saving time and preventing errors in the final execution. Your power of mental visualization is the most important creative skill you can develop, but it can be enhanced by a greater perspective and an awareness and knowledge of other disciplines.

Alternatively, no matter how good you are at simulating what your project entails, it's been my experience that whenever you do something new for the first time there is a hidden tuition payment. Anyone that has attended college understands that the price is hefty. Knowledge isn't given out for free. But finishing college doesn't mean an end to tuition payments. I have learned over the years that whenever I do something new, there is always an unexpected cost. Think of it as an embedded toll that's collected in one form or another. Nothing can take the place of experience, but sometimes a critical piece of information or knowledge can help us discern hidden complications. I mention this to alert the reader that even after graduation, there's no end to the ways we invest in education; sometimes those imposed payments are manageable, and other times they can be cost-prohibitive.

The Payoff

College is an excellent place to enrich your life and discover many new topics and ideas. The college experience is full of opportunities for exploration. Typically, you can find whatever you're seeking in college. If you are looking for a good time, you are almost guaranteed to find it. If you are looking for lifelong friends and relationships, you can probably find them, too. If you wish to pursue an interest in academic study, this is easily done, because college certainly can be centered on the joy of learning. But if you are looking for a livelihood, a professional career, or a way to comfortably support yourself and your family in the future, you can find this too. You can achieve your loftiest goals if you are willing to apply yourself and seriously make academic study a priority.

But people's perspective about college has changed in the last decade. What if college isn't all it's cracked up to be? What's the real value of a college degree anymore? There are some obstacles in the path ahead and knowing about them can help you prepare to deal with them. One of these is the gap between college expectations and what college actually delivers; another is the problem of subpar professors and other hidden hazards. If you know how to compensate for these issues, you can prepare yourself.

PART II

Bumps in the Road

GETTING STARTED ON A NEW journey can be energizing, but what happens when you encounter bumps in the road? How do you prepare for the unexpected? Author Edith Wharton once wryly observed, "The turnings of life seldom show a sign-post; or rather, though the sign is always there, it is usually placed some distance back, like the notices that give warning of a bad hill or a level railway-crossing."

Most students entering college don't see certain warning signs along the path. The signposts are "some distance back" from the road and are difficult to make out unless you know to look for them. Here I'm hoping to point out some of the major problems in pursuing a college education to give you a heads-up. In this section you'll learn what to look out for—pitfalls that lie in wait for unsuspecting travelers—and how to avoid certain calamities on the journey ahead.

Even if you heed all these warnings, though, I want to let you know that things still may not always go smoothly. We'll talk about what happens if you encounter an unexpected setback—in other words, what to expect when the unexpected happens.

CHAPTER 3

Don't Fall into the Gap

The Problem with Advanced Education

"In truth, elite education has become a cattle brand. It signifies lots of things other than knowledge."
– VICTOR DAVIS HANSON[16]

The Gap Between Student Expectations and College Education

We've all been conditioned to think that a college degree is the gateway to success and happiness. Higher education has always been viewed as the first step toward a better life. Conduct a search on the Internet, and you'll see story after story on the importance of a college degree. It seems the benefits are legion. But is it really all it's cracked up to be?

The first bump you'll probably encounter is one that's nearly impossible to see, unless someone points it out to you. That is, you can easily trip and fall into the huge gap between your expectations about college and the reality of what a college education can provide.

There's a rarely discussed chasm between what students expect and what colleges deliver. The disparity is compounded by differences in perspective. Students think college is not only going to assist them in developing a profession but also provide education, insights, and information on navigating life after school. This perception leads students to rely on colleges to launch their careers, even though a college education doesn't prepare them for adulthood. Yes, you'll sometimes find departments or advisors focused on "career readiness," but these hardly compare to how you'll be cutting your teeth in the real world.

College curriculums are simply not set up to provide the fundamental training and practical application required by most professions. The vast majority of courses are mired in theory and concepts, with little offered in the way of useful, real-world application. This creates a disparity between what higher education supplies and the skills and insights that the post-college world demands.

The realization of a job and career is left to the student to figure out on their own, occasionally with help from parents, friends, and acquaintances. It's amazing that colleges have succeeded in convincing parents that a degree offers the key to a successful life. To be sure, it does have benefits. It typically creates a student community, and that's worth something in today's society. College also provides time for introspection and collaboration. It can help students establish their perspectives and goals through exposure to concepts, ideas, and important writings. But a college degree is *not* a foolproof launching pad for your career.

All too often a new degree makes a graduate feel like they have accomplished something that gives them a significant edge. And while the pursuit of knowledge is commendable, that newly minted degree can result in an unhealthy dose of hubris. In truth, a college education doesn't prepare you for navigating life outside of the classroom, and it probably never will.

Learning the Hard Way

I graduated with a BS in Chemistry with a minor in Business. I'm not saying I expected a job to be handed to me on a silver platter, but I thought some reasonable effort would lead to at least a handful of job offers to choose from. Instead, after several months, I had no prospects. I searched for almost a year, had some interviews, and aimed lower and lower. Finally, I ended up with the opportunity to work as a retail assistant. I was told not to be discouraged; the economy was lousy at the time. But how could I accept putting in so much time, money, and effort to land a job that I could have gotten with a high school diploma?

I bailed out of the job market and decided to go to graduate school instead. I was accepted into the biochemistry nutrition department on a research assistant scholarship. It's good to be resourceful, but it's bad to forestall the inevitable.

In graduate school, I noticed a similar pattern among the demeanor and behavior of professors. They were intelligent and knowledgeable in their field but completely lacking in other ways. It was as though they had limited exposure to interpersonal skills, capitalism, free markets, and the workplace. After graduating, I decided I'd had enough of research and lab work.

I was going for the sure thing and would continue my studies to get an MBA; what could be a better program to launch myself into a career and adulthood, I thought.

There I found some professors who came from the private sector, and they appeared to have a connection to the real world. Even so, the curriculum fell short on specifics.

A Recent Study Suggests Students Feel Unprepared for a Career

According to a College Pulse survey carried out by LendEDU, nearly 40 percent of graduating college seniors feel unprepared for their future careers.[17] What's more shocking is that the survey found students going into college as freshmen felt more prepared for a career than graduating seniors leaving with a degree.

The 2018 survey asked 7,749 college students from six colleges and universities: "Do you think that college is sufficiently preparing you for your future career?" And 40 percent felt unprepared. The problem is that instead of learning critical life skills—such as how to manage money, negotiate, or communicate and write well—kids are mostly taught to memorize information and review theory. This type of learning comes at the expense of learning critical life skills—which parents are generally expected to teach. But many parents aren't qualified or the family dynamics don't allow for education to take place. Alternatively, advanced education could be the perfect setting for young people to learn these indispensable skills.

Smart Kids

Currently in school, the "smartest" students are the ones who are best at memorizing information. These are the skills that are emphasized at the expense of soft skills—creativity, problem-solving, and presentation—in which many of the "less smart" students excel. The supposedly "smart" students actually *need* to develop soft skills, which are far more valuable in the real world than the ability to recall the Pythagorean theorem. In adulthood generally, and work specifically, soft skills are much more important than the amount of information you've memorized—which is why the old adage "It's not what you know, it's who you know" exists—so why don't schools reflect this reality?

If we were to audit the American education system, I guarantee it would find test after test focused on memorized content, and very little emphasis on assessing or developing soft skills.

I can't understand why advanced education doesn't even attempt to teach kids the core skills needed to live in the real world. Why is college thought of so highly when it lacks training in personal growth, financial management, communications, emotional intelligence, and healthy living? Psychology comes the closest to providing some interpersonal skills, but it's usually optional. This leads us to the other problem in education; namely that teachers and professors operate in separate silos of discipline without any thought to the integration of studies.

Why Is a College Education So Ill-Suited to the Challenge?

The quality of college faculty you are likely to encounter is inconsistent. While there are many great professors in higher education, you need to jettison any presumption you may have that they necessarily know more than you do about real life beyond their specialty of study. Most students automatically defer to the authority and superior knowledge of their teachers. What's important to notice, though, is that instructors are human, too, and given to big egos and foibles just like everybody else. There are some professors who, though arguably very knowledgeable in their field, are nearly useless in teaching students anything about how the real world works. I call these folks "hedgehogs," which I will explain further.

It takes a certain kind of talent and imagination to bolster a curriculum and make it relevant. We tend to rely on college professors to do that, but our faith is often misplaced. Most professors are intelligent and gifted experts in their respective fields, but they often seem to come with severe limitations. This fits squarely with Jung's observation: "A special ability means a heavy expenditure of energy in a particular direction, with a consequent drain from some other side of life."

In other words, some professors are like gifted prodigies whose skills are highly developed in a particular field. Their insatiable passion for a particular subject has led them to give that area of study specialized attention at the expense of other obligations. They may even have neglected development in other areas of life because of this singular focus. In some instances, you may find that they have limited interpersonal skills, difficulty making eye contact, and a limited ability to appreciate social cues. They may be introverted, preferring to hide out in ivory towers rather than navigate the halls of business and enterprise.

In contrast, senior business executives make eye contact, confront problems, and hold people accountable, and they don't put up with fools. Their social skills and ability to interact with staff are every bit as good as their knowledge of the business enterprise. Not so with many college professors, and yet we entrust professors to teach our students. Worse, we implicitly assume the students will learn from them how to navigate life.

Beware of Highly Specialized Hedgehogs

Lest you think I'm being unduly harsh in my criticism of professors, consider this description of limited-focus experts by psychologist and political scientist Philip Tetlock. Tetlock decided to put political and economic experts and their predictions to the test. At the height of the Cold War between the United States and the Soviet Union, he collected forecasts from 284 highly educated experts who averaged more than 12 years of experience in their specialties. To ensure that the predictions were concrete, experts had to give specific probabilities of future events. The project lasted 20 years and comprised 82,361 probability estimates about the future.

The result of the study demonstrated that the experts were, by and large, horrific forecasters. Their areas of specialty, years of experience, and—for some—access to classified information made no difference. They were bad at short-term forecasting and bad at long-term forecasting. Even when faced with their results, many experts never admitted systematic flaws in their judgment because they were so heavily invested in their theories. This is the classic behavior of a single-focus thinker.

One subgroup of scholars, however, did manage to see more of what was coming—multi-disciplined individuals not vested in a single subject who pulled from each argument and integrated contradictory worldviews. They agreed that Gorbachev was a real reformer *and* that the Soviet Union had lost legitimacy outside Russia. A few of those integrators saw that the end of the Soviet Union was close at hand and that real reforms would be the catalyst.

The integrators outperformed their colleagues in pretty much every way but especially trounced them on long-term predictions. Tetlock assigned nicknames (borrowed from the philosopher Isaiah Berlin) to the experts he'd observed: The highly specialized hedgehogs knew "one big thing," while the integrator foxes knew "many little things."

Here's a case in point that illustrates the hedgehog problem. In 1968, Paul Ehrlich, a professor at Stanford University, wrote his bestselling book, *The Population Bomb*. In it, he predicted a doomsday apocalypse resulting from overpopulation. Resource shortages would cause hundreds of millions of starvation deaths within a decade. It was based on cold, hard math: The human population was growing exponentially; the food supply was not. He knew that nature did not regulate animal populations delicately. When animal populations explode, blowing past available resources, they crash. As it turns out, Ehrlich's prediction was almost comically bad because humans can harness science to change the limitations set by nature.

Hedgehogs are tightly focused. Some have spent their career studying one problem. Like Ehrlich, they fashion tidy theories of how the world works based on observations made through the single lens of their specialty. Foxes, meanwhile, "draw from an eclectic array of traditions, and accept ambiguity and contradiction," Tetlock wrote. Where hedgehogs represent narrow depth, foxes embody breadth.[18]

A Hedgehog Gone Wild

What happens when you combine academic intelligence with instinctual sociopath behavior? Take the case of Paul de Man, a shadowy Belgian figure who immigrated to the United States in 1948.[19] He was an imposter who excelled at convincing gullible intellectuals to take him under their wing.

In fact, that's exactly how he got his first job upon arrival. He met a New York City socialite and fellow intellectual, who found him to be sophisticated and *tres chic* (very cool). She helped him get a teaching job at Bard College. De Man duly provided a fabricated résumé, listing an imaginary master's thesis and doctoral thesis. To add to his liberal mystique, he described himself as a resistance fighter during the war. De Man demonstrated the ultimate cynicism by co-opting the fresh and horrific memory left by Nazis and Fascists to serve in his deception. This later proved to be particularly problematic when the truth came out decades later.

Unfortunately, the newly minted instructor, de Man, failed to pay his rent for more than a year while teaching at Bard and was summarily dismissed. Ultimately, it didn't matter; his stint at Bard was the foundation for establishing himself in US academia. Armed with an understanding of liberal academic naiveté and his evolving ability to doctor documents, de Man was admitted into the PhD program in comparative literature at Harvard University. Chased by immigration officials, he left the country, returning voluntarily to Europe in the middle of his studies. Two years later he returned and, despite some shortcomings, was awarded his degree. By 1960, de Man had taught at three prestigious universities: Cornell, Johns Hopkins, and Yale. He eventually became a full professor of French and comparative literature from 1970 until his death in 1983, at age 65. Several years later, the truth came out. He had collaborated with the Nazis; was an admitted fascist, anti-Semite, and ex-con; and was a twice-convicted felon—first for being a Nazi sympathizer and later for forgery and theft, which is why he left Europe in the first place. Later, they discovered he was also a polygamist, having both an American wife and a European wife and family; not to mention that he was also a truly self-absorbed and absent father.

De Man appeared to live by the philosophy that the ends justify the means, leaving a trail of victims that spanned two continents. Some might characterize him as a sociopath, others might say that he expressed a keen skill of portraying himself as an unusual or eccentric personality, markedly different from his true self. Either way, one must admit, given his journey in life, he displayed remarkable skill—his survival instincts were second to none.

The problem with hedgehogs and geniuses is that they demonstrate commitment, but that commitment is often unrestrained and at the expense of everything else. Hedgehogs have an insatiable preoccupation with their single-minded interest and are unable to give in measure to their personal lives.

I mention these stories because we tend to glorify genius, but it typically comes with baggage and even hazards. Yet we entrust professors to teach our students, and we implicitly assume they will teach the students how to navigate life.

The Difference Between Education and Indoctrination

Another danger to be aware of is that higher education is often laced with indoctrination. Some indoctrination is supplied under the approval of the institution, while other forms of indoctrination are propagated by fellow students and others affiliated with the university, though what they are offering may not be sanctioned by the college.

Academic ivory towers aren't content to prepare young minds, encourage academic excellence, and develop students' skills. Often academic institutions express a noble higher cause; their purpose is to discover new truths and transmit those truths to the masses. Unfortunately, many of these so-called truths work only in theory.

But college also exposes students to indoctrination artists. These are calculating recruiters who focus on single issues; they specialize in inspiring the gullible to be their street warriors for a cause of their choosing. They typically offer simplistic solutions to a very complex set of circumstances, but their passion can be contagious. Whatever you do, don't fall for it. In one's youthful enthusiasm, the difference between right and wrong seems to be based on simplistic premises, and any deviation from them is a willful disregard for humanity. But the reality is that life is more nuanced, filled with shades of grey and laced with unintended consequences. Life is far more complex with many forces in play.

Preparing for the Real World

Colleges have succeeded in convincing parents that they offer the key to success in life—yet they're staffed by hedgehogs. Think of a typical college professor: very intelligent and extremely knowledgeable but only usually in their limited area of expertise. In fact, most colleges are swimming in faculty that Tetlock would probably describe as hedgehogs. Many of them are gifted in their own way, but they are also inherently flawed. An ivory tower is the ideal place for gifted people with tunnel vision and limited social skills. It can serve as a sanctuary for these individuals, as well as a place for higher learning.

Over the years, the college sales pitch progressively expanded from career education to imply that you will be given the skills to equip you for a successful life. But the idea that a college faculty composed mostly of hedgehogs is going to teach you how to successfully navigate life is ludicrous.

The reality is that graduating students will ultimately enter an asymmetrical world, a free market economy driven by businesses where performance, not theory, passes muster and makes the difference between success or failure. Your goal in going to college should be to become smart as a fox, someone with a breadth of study and understanding, someone who integrates many smaller insights and areas of interest into a workable understanding of the way things actually work. It's up to you to figure out how to round out your higher learning experience so you'll be prepared for the real world.

Limits of Education—the Dyatlov Pass Mystery

As you launch your career, you first need to accept and understand the limits of education. The problem with a college education is that it gives the impression that it prepares you for life, when in reality, it doesn't. Your college education is woefully inadequate if it doesn't encourage strategic and tactical moves. Education should include developing the expertise to find the high ground and gain perspective.

The Dyatlov Pass mystery is a story that exemplifies how you can be the brightest and best, have a terrific education, and still be vulnerable to the slings and arrows of outrageous fortune.[20]

More than 60 years ago, a group of extraordinary Russian students, seven men and two women, decided to go on a camping trip in the middle of a Russian winter. Many of the students were in their final year, ready to graduate and full of promise and ambition. This was to be their last adventure together as students.

They were going to undertake a three-week cross-country skiing trek near the Russian Ural Mountains. But before they could undertake such a trek, they had to meet rigorous requirements set by the university's exploration club and academia.

Gaining approval, one of the women sent a letter along the way, writing, "We are going camping, nine of us, and it's a great bunch of people. I have all the warm clothes I need, so don't worry about me!" It was supposed to be a three-week trek, covering 200 miles in the winter of 1959. The three weeks passed, and the students' parents didn't hear anything from their sons and daughters. They knew something was wrong.

Searchers converged on the area and found their bodies spread over a wide area. Their bodies were partially clothed, some had no shoes and some of the bodies were badly mutilated and burned. What happened that caused them to abandon their tent in terror? As one of Russia's most enduring mysteries, it spawned all sorts of conspiracy theories as varied as a *military cover-up*, a *UFO sighting*, an *abominable snowman* attack, *radiation fallout* from secret weapons tests, and a clash with the indigenous *Mansi people*.

But scientists may finally have unraveled the 60-year mystery surrounding the nine students' demise. The answer may lie in an elegant computer model based on surprising sources. On their journey, the students encountered a winter storm with high winds. To protect their tent from the wind, they decided to cut into the mountain snow to form a barrier. Swiss geotechnical engineers theorize that their tent was hit by a slab of snow in the middle of the night. In their panic, they cut through their tent to escape being buried by the snow. Scientists used historical records to recreate the mountain's environment on the night of the incident and simulated a slab avalanche, by analyzing snow friction. Their research provided this more sensible explanation, drawing on advanced computer modeling to posit that an unusually timed avalanche sealed the hikers' fate.[21]

The accumulation of a little knowledge can be a dangerous thing, but no matter how well they planned their expedition, nothing could have prepared them for such an event! Nature is a cruel taskmaster that is slow to release its secrets.

This story underscores the inherent asymmetrical aspects of life and how vulnerable we are! Nature sets the rules and we either defy or compensate for them, but as a product of nature, we can be just as unpredictable.

Is a College Education Worth the Investment?

After reading about the huge gap between what we expect from college and what it actually delivers, as well as the limitations of narrowly focused professors and the unpredictable asymmetrical aspects of life, you might wonder if it's actually worth going to college. This question is often taken up in the media.

The narrative usually begins with this question: "Is a college education worth the investment?" Folks who just read the headlines or rely on the opinion pages for their information might conclude that the value of a college degree is in decline. The facts tell a different story.

Contrary to this false narrative, a college education is more important now than ever before, for both tangible and intangible reasons. A college degree is still the surest way to increase wage potential. In addition, with the rise of artificial intelligence and the consistent call for multi-talented and flexible critical thinkers in the workplace, college is—and will increasingly be—the best way to prepare for an uncertain future.

College offers benefits beyond the classroom. The campus setting at a college counts for a lot. It provides a community for students. The environment can provide time for introspection and collaborative interactions. It can help students formulate new ideas and goals through exposure to other concepts and important writings, since a college degree isn't a fail-proof launching pad for a student's career.

This inherent value of campus life is lost for online colleges. Undergraduates have been raised to expect a college experience, not just an education. Part of it is the fun factor, of course. But part of it is also functional. Classmates form friendships and become part of each other's professional networks.

Students have the opportunity to learn in physical spaces, like science labs. They get a chance to mature in a relatively consequence-free environment, where a callow 18-year-old can do the sorts of things callow 18-year-olds do without landing in serious legal trouble, and they learn how to deal with college authority figures face-to-face. It's a long process of acculturation that transitions students into the adult world, probably with the help of a very expensive-to-maintain social and career services department.

In the real world, math is not something you do in isolation; neither is science, history, or the arts. It requires collaboration. The campus setting offered by academia can help condition students to the importance of collaboration.

Colleges offer prospective employers a sort of third-party validation, or a stamp of qualification of their graduates. For high-profile colleges, a diploma is a giant seal of approval for certain employers, effectively signaling to the business community that this student is an achiever. This is important because companies don't have time to interview every single applicant for a job and interrogate their actual skills. They need a shortcut to tell whether a 22-year-old is actually worth talking to, which is why, despite anti-college evangelists like venture capitalist Peter Thiel, Silicon Valley companies are still looking for candidates with a degree.

So, What Good Is That Sheepskin Diploma?

What is it that a college diploma actually provides? I contend that it's a certification that signals to prospective employers that you have been screened, evaluated, and tested. It indicates to certain employers that you are, at a minimum, a viable candidate.

Being young and inexperienced can have its advantages in the job application process. Employers are not very good at spotting talent, so they assume that every young candidate is potentially gifted and talented. Typically, the staff responsible for screening candidates don't have confidence in their own judgment to discern the good from the mediocre or the bad. The other challenge for recruiters is that the qualities that have the greatest impact on success are typically latent and difficult to measure—traits like discipline, the ability to maintain composure, leadership abilities. Most latent talents are typically discovered on the frontline under duress. Consequently, a large corporation will hire more young candidates than they need, but it invariably means being subjected to a culling process.

The interview serves as a preliminary culling process. Employers are trying to discern the candidate's makeup and character in this first meeting. They're also trying to determine suitability for the job and whether your personality and sensibilities are a fit for the organization. A great first impression must include selling oneself while telegraphing the notion that you want to be part of a team.

When you're young and just starting your career, people are more likely to give you the benefit of the doubt. When you're older with a track record and years of experience, you'll find there is less tolerance for responding inappropriately to questions. It's all about projecting a positive attitude and a sense of commitment with energy and professionalism. Then you must prove you're worth keeping around—or figure out how to make yourself a valued employee. Alternatively, the prospective employer is looking for distinguishing cues and factors that are unique to the candidate, such as a diploma from a prestigious university. This is important in the event the candidate turns out to be a dud, and the person selecting that candidate needs to find cover for their decision.

The Advantages of American Higher Education

Even though students often encounter a gap between what they expect from college and what it delivers, it's also important to emphasize the uniqueness of the American higher education system. While it's true that you must be able to navigate the system to your advantage, its openness and flexibility makes it possible for students (emerging adults) to take college courses covering a broad range of subjects. It's really an amazing maze, yours for the wandering!

The college campus allows students to hone their interpersonal skills. These include what I refer to as soft skills: the ability to understand personality types and emotional intelligence traits that help people interact well with others, such as collaboration, communication, punctuality, and leadership. Social skills can't be memorized as content. They are largely intangible skills that need to be developed through practice. Overall, social skills such as persuasion, emotional intelligence, and a talent for teaching others are in high demand across industries—more so than narrow technical skills. If you're from a family that didn't "do feelings," these interpersonal relationship muscles may not have been developed. This is an opportunity to cultivate those muscles.

Further, you can strengthen these skills on and off throughout your twenties and beyond. The US education system allows students to explore and see how they might fit into society. Academic pursuit is important, but to maximize your investment you must also take advantage of resources such as social and psychological services, personality testing, matching of suitable careers with personality types, and guidance in transitioning into adulthood or career placement services, as we have mentioned.

Even if you succeed in adjusting your expectations to what college can actually deliver and achieve an awareness of hedgehogs, there are still additional hidden hazards that lurk along the college trail. That's the focus of our next chapter.

CHAPTER 4

Hidden Hazards

"I've never let my school interfere with my education."

– MARK TWAIN

WHEN CANDIDATES LOOK FOR OR consider a college, they often miss many of the potential pitfalls. After all, it's an opportunity, right? If we work hard, show perseverance, and put in the hours, isn't it all upside at graduation? Yes and no. While graduation is certainly one of the payoffs, hard work and stamina are not the only price you pay. There is huge economic input into higher education, and some of the hidden hazards of gaining a college education reflect this reality. Getting a worthwhile college experience involves you in a costly transaction, and that means you must become aware that many colleges are not solely fixated on helping you make the right choices. They're more interested in helping you make the choice that they may want you to make.

Fortunately, there are clues, but they are easier to spot once you realize that, for many in the process, your college application is not just a rite of passage or a special test or even a natural progression of your education. In college admissions departments, your application is more like a sales inquiry. I'm not mincing words here. It's a transaction, and like any transaction, the warning of *caveat emptor* (buyer beware) applies.

Beware the Slick Sales Pitch

One hidden hazard in your college trail is the slick recruitment sales pitch. Be smart; don't fall for it. By now, you've probably started talking to people about college options and maybe even gotten onto recruitment lists from various colleges seeking to lure you to their schools. Colleges are savvy marketers, and if you ask about one, you're likely to be targeted by many others too. You may have already found your mailbox inundated with shiny college brochures or your inbox barraged with college emails trying in every possible way to snag your attention. How do you sift through all that marketing material so you can make an appropriate choice?

One way is by knowing a few secrets about what you're looking at and understanding how the college game is played—that is, how colleges go about selling you a success story.

One measure of success for an institution of higher learning is how many of its graduates achieve fame and success. Colleges and universities have been successful in selling their version of alumni success. In their argument, the institution takes ownership of the success of their graduates to imply to the graduates that they'd better be grateful to the institution and that they are successful because they attended a prestigious university (Stanford, Yale, Harvard, Penn, Princeton, or MIT, for example). It further implies that graduates were nothing, with no chance at success, until they attended the institution. It robs the graduate of their own agency, giving the institution all the credit.

Panning for Gold

Colleges and universities will exploit their exclusivity to be selective in the students they accept. I call it panning for gold. For example, Ivy League colleges only accept about 6 percent of applicants, but this distillation of applicants really amounts to distillation upon distillation. Most average students are discouraged from applying. High SAT score requirements combined with a laborious application process are designed to discourage academically average students from applying. Consequently, the applicants that do apply already represent a highly skewed population of top-tier academic performing students. Exclusive colleges and universities have the luxury of selecting from the best of the best.

Moreover, prestigious educational institutions have the luxury of attracting legacy candidates, sons and daughters from wealthy families, or the offspring of powerful political figures. Bush family members have a history of attending Yale, while Kennedy family offspring seem to have an easy time of gaining admission to Harvard. Other political figures such as the Clintons, who graduated from Yale Law School, were able to navigate their daughter to getting accepted to Stanford University. No doubt, she was also accepted at Yale, but having visited both campuses over the years, I, too, would have selected the Palo Alto campus over the gritty, grimy New Haven setting of Yale University. The beauty of accepting legacy students is that they're primed for success. They're already famous, and when they graduate, they're destined to have the wind behind their sails. It gives considerable confirmation to the old saying, "it's not what you know, it's who you know."

Effectively, exclusive universities can stack the deck in their favor, since most institutions realize that one of the most important parameters of a great alma mater is the quality of its alumni. One way to evaluate the legacy of a great university or an educational institute is by studying their alumni. The larger the community of successful alumni, the more famous the university or college becomes. With each successful alum, the name of the institution slowly and gradually becomes bigger, and over time, it becomes so famous that students from all over the world want to attend.

To illustrate how colleges and universities feature their alumni, I have selected three institutions of higher learning that each represents a distinct category of institution: Bard College, a small, specialized college; Duke University, an elite, private university; and Purdue University, a large, public university.

Bard College

Bard is a small college 90 miles north of New York City on the banks of the Hudson River. Total enrollment is 1,200 students. I'm quite familiar with Bard because I grew up near the Hudson River about 40 miles to the south. Founded in 1860 originally as St. Stephen's College by John Bard in association with leaders of New York City Episcopal Church, it was established as an all men's school concentrating on classical curricula. In 1928, St. Stephen's became an undergraduate school of Columbia University, and under the leadership of Dean Donald G. Tewksbury, Bard further integrated the classical and progressive educational traditions, in the process becoming the first college in the nation to give full academic status to the study of the creative and performing arts. In 1934, the name of the college was changed to Bard in honor of its founder. It began coeducation in the 1940s. Historically, student enrollment was under 1,000 students.

The typical Bard student marches to the beat of a different drummer, as evidenced by its alumni, which are largely made up of creative types: entertainers, comedians, writers, artists, and iconoclasts. According to stereotypes, artists compared to scientists are less rigid and possibly less rational, yet more embracing of creativity. This led to Bard becoming one of the first institutions to embrace a pass-fail option.

The beauty of majoring in artistic endeavors is that they're an expression of personal feelings and emotions. Some might say that art and its assessment is subjective, while others might say that artistic judgments are not purely subjective at all. There are many judgments that some people make about visual art that are related to long-established objective standards about composition, painting techniques in the various media, and the effective use of materials.

Bard's most famous graduates are largely entertainers of some sort. While some are truly gifted, others mostly possess a high Q Score (a television term that means that the camera seems to like them), which draws an audience.

- Donald Fagen, musician, and co-founder of Steely Dan
- Jonah Hill, actor

- Gia Coppola, film director, granddaughter of Francis Ford Coppola
- Chevy Chase, comedian, actor, and famous SNL comedian
- Larry Hagman, actor, son of actress Mary Martin, famous for playing Peter Pan
- Ali Wentworth, actor, comedian, married to ABC News anchor George Stephanopoulos
- Ronan Farrow, journalist and the son of Mia Farrow and Woody Allen

By and large, students who attend have a passion for the arts and typically came from well-to-do, privileged families. Many of these graduates are from metropolitan areas, including New York City. It caters to artists and writers who may not want to be exposed to strict competitive academic performance but would rather focus on the arts and the challenge of being an artist and harness their creativity and spontaneity, which drives an artistic career.

Duke University

There is a certain irony to the patronage of Duke University. It was built on the largess of the Duke fortune, created from the success of Reynolds Tobacco Company. Duke has a total enrollment of over 15,000 students, but only 6,600 undergraduates. The medical school is part of the main campus, which explains the significantly lower undergrad enrollment relative to total students. Founded by Methodists and Quakers in 1838, it was later endowed by the Duke family.

Duke typically receives a total of 40,000 or more

undergraduate applications with an acceptance rate of approximately 6 percent. Some people call Duke the Harvard of the South, meaning that it has been very effective in establishing its academic standing. Over the years, it has employed 15 Nobel laureates, largely in medicine, chemistry, and physics.

The school has a long list of accomplished alumni, too numerous to review. The most notable graduates include:

- Richard Nixon, law school graduate and 37th President of the United States
- Melinda Gates, the co-founder of one of the largest charitable foundations in the world
- Tim Cook, CEO of Apple

Additionally, it boasts ten US Senators, 24 congress members, half a dozen governors, 20 or more cabinet members, and numerous judges as graduates of Duke.

Purdue

On the flat plains of the Midwest, dominated by cornfields as far as the eye can see, there is an oasis of a town, Lafayette, Indiana, where Purdue University is situated. It has a total enrollment of 41,000 students, with an undergraduate enrollment of 32,672. The university was founded in 1869 after Lafayette, Indiana, businessman John Purdue donated the land and money to establish a college of science, technology, and agriculture in his name.

As a public university, Purdue can't compete with elite colleges in recruiting top-tier student talent. It must compete by developing a franchise of some sort. It's known for its engineering and applied science prowess; it churns out thousands of engineering graduates. It also offers a specialty field of study in aeronautical and astronautical engineering. Consequently, Purdue is also known as the cradle of astronauts. It has graduated 24 NASA astronauts, including some of the first to walk on the moon.

Individual Talent Trumps College Attended

The truth of the matter is that ambitious, hardworking, intelligent young people will be successful no matter where they go to school. The secret is that elite schools just tend to attract more of them. There's a selection bias enjoyed by elite schools. Many of the people who apply and qualify are those who are likely to be successful no matter where they go to college or what path they pursue in life. But elite colleges and universities are very adept at keeping up the façade that they are the ones creating successful people, and they are responsible for maintaining the focus of their students and making sure that students meet certain expectations.

After studying the career records of nearly 1,000 graduates of the Harvard Business School, for example, Professor Gordon L. Marshall concluded that "academic success and business achievement have relatively little association with each other."[22]

To reach this conclusion, he sought without success to find a correlation between grades and such measures of achievement as title, salary, and a person's own satisfaction with their career progress. (Only in the case of grades in elective courses was a significant correlation found.) In other words, what a student learns about management in graduate school, as measured by the grades they receive, does not equip them to build a successful career in business.

Scholastic standing in undergraduate school is an equally unreliable guide to an individual's management potential. Professor Eugene E. Jennings of the University of Michigan has conducted research which shows that "the routes to the top are apt to hold just as many or more who graduated below the highest one third of their college class than above (on a per capita basis)."[23]

A great many executives who mistakenly believe that grades are a valid measure of leadership potential have expressed concern that fewer and fewer of those "top-third" graduates from the better-known colleges and universities are embarking on careers in business. What these executives do not recognize, however, is that academic ability does not assure that an individual will be able to learn what they need to know to build a career in fields that involve leading, changing, developing, or working with people. An overreliance on scholastic learning ability may have caused leading universities and business organizations to reject a percentage of those who have had the greatest potential for creativity and growth in non-academic careers.

A Cautionary Tale

As noted, the college sales pitch implies that you'll learn the skills to equip you for a successful life, and the typical young prospective college recruit is an easy target for this pitch. A college education can indeed have great value, but it cannot teach you all the skills you need to prepare you for life in the real world. Hermann Hesse's story, *Beneath the Wheel* (also called *The Prodigy*), makes the point tragically but powerfully:

Hans, a gifted student, spent his entire youth in a peaceful but insular Southern Bavarian village.[24] The residents discovered that he was an exceptionally gifted student. In their community pride, they pressed him onto a path of serious scholarship.

Hans dutifully followed, going off to attain higher education, where he was subjected to a regimen of study and endless examinations; his success was rewarded only with more crushing assignments. Having left his village, he met new people who were just as gifted or talented. He befriended a rebellious young poet. To be a good poet, one has to live and experience life to the fullest. He began to imagine other possibilities outside of scholarship and academia. But this created inner conflict and distracted him from his studies. Failing, he was sent home after a nervous breakdown. Initially, Hans was revived by nature and romance and vowed never to return to the gray conformity of academia. Back in his village, he followed tradition and subjected himself to an apprenticeship. Too intelligent for a menial job, but not gifted enough or motivated enough to achieve the scholarship required to join the ranks of academia, he ended his life.

Some people reading this story may say he was a victim of a rigid society. I say poor Hans failed to focus on his personal development and failed to gain perspective that only comes with finding the high ground to be able to perceive and understand a multi-faceted world. In a way, he never left the confines of his small village, but he also placed too much reliance on his education to offer up the insights to successfully navigate life. Higher education offers the illusion of higher learning, but in reality, it offers little practical application for dealing with day-to-day challenges.

College Selection Can and Will Have Consequences

When I was a newly-arrived college freshman, I was totally unprepared. Relative to my classmates who grew up in suburbia or New York City, I was out of my element, unaware of basic cultural understandings. I considered attending Bard College. What attracted me was the prospect of scholarships and grant money. Plus, it stood in stark contrast to the large, impersonal university setting, which usually comes with overcrowding in the first year, a lack of dormitory space, and reliance on large lecture halls which can signify "the impersonal multiversity." Given the conflicting goals of most universities, there is the appearance of lack of attention to undergraduate education and an inherent emphasis on graduate studies and research.

What I learned over time is that the college selection decision is far more complex, and it can—and will—have consequences for your life. The people in a class can be from all over the country, and it's the first time they've all been brought together. But they all have one thing in common: the college they selected. For example, Bard College, because of its small size, had to narrow its curriculum, concentrating on the arts and humanities rather than science or engineering. Therefore, the selection of Bard College means associating with classmates made up largely of artist and creative types. I know it's a stereotype, but the perception that scientists are a bit more rigid and less artistic while artists are less rational than the rest of us does have real world merits. Sometimes described as the left side of the brain versus the right side—or simply logical thinking versus artistic creativity—the two are often seen as opposites. How often do you see artists who need affirmation and need to be in front of an audience?

It's healthy for colleges to narrow their curriculum and home in on their franchise, but colleges that focus on real world skills, including soft skills, will offer their students an advantage that will give their graduating class an edge in the job market and in navigating life.

I also discovered that children of affluent, talented parents come with a perspective and lifestyle that can seriously conflict with someone never exposed to such a world. I have learned that what appears on the surface is generally far from the truth. Children of rich, well-educated parents, who have attended elite prep schools, can show serious levels of maladjustments, displaying troubling behavior that worsens in college. Their behavior usually involves alcohol and marijuana and can also decline into serious drug abuse as a way to dull their psychological problems. I met students that admitted to undergoing the psychological evaluation that too often comes with a privileged lifestyle.

Those engaged in destructive behavior are always looking for fresh recruits to affirm their choices, and at a vulnerable age, I didn't need to be exposed to that kind of behavior. In my case, there was zero tolerance for screwing up.

My parents came from modest means. I had no access to a support network, meaning that I had no access to a second chance. At the same time, I desperately needed to exit my small-town, narrow-minded, insular existence.

I later concluded that I was an introvert. And to be part of a student body of extroverts could have been a disaster. As an introvert, to be thrust into a student body made up of artistic extraverts would have been incredibly confusing and distracting from serious education. Much later I learned that artists, in their effort to cultivate their creative side, need to stay in touch with their inner child, while I desperately needed to develop my adult side, along with a healthy dose of emotional maturity. I was particularly vulnerable because I was a naïve youth, trying to find myself along with finding my individual north star upon which to navigate life. I went to a marginal high school in the backcountry of Upstate New York. To say that I was young and impressionable is an understatement. At home, we had only a handful of books, and most were on hunting and fishing.

Today when I think of the typical Bard College student, I'm reminded of Woody Allen's one line summation of a character in his movie, *Annie Hall*: "You're like New York, Jewish, left-wing, liberal, intellectual, Central Park West, Brandeis University, the socialist summer camps and the, the father with the Ben Shahn drawings, right, and the really, y'know, strike-oriented kind." Ironically, Woody Allen's character had a crush on her, but as the writer, he was most likely projecting his own liberal views and perspective onto his character in the movie and straddling a whole New York City ethnic group with this political mindset.

It's the kind of mentality that comes with a talented person who knows they possess a unique genius that will attract an audience—or someone who knows that they will inherit a trust fund. In some ways, it's not a coincidence that his son Ronan Farrow went to school there. I could have found myself being swept up in some countercultural movement and distracted from serious academic study with no second chances. At that time I hadn't read *Beneath the Wheel*, but I could have been led down an unnatural, possibly toxic, path of irresponsible behavior and become enveloped in self-indulging counterculture myopia that mirrored Hans' story, ending up isolated from my roots and the people that I relied on for support.

Hidden Hazards in Your Freshman Year

The challenges new college students face range from minor nuisances to undermining distractions. Invariably it starts with freshman student overcrowding and large, impersonal classes.

In the first year of college, there's so much information to absorb and comprehend, it feels like you're drinking from a firehose. It can be stressful having to select from a wide array of courses (both required and elective), screen professors, and schedule around conflicts, all while having to take full custody of your personal life for the first time. The intensity of the experience can be quite overwhelming. Anxiety-ridden students scurry around trying to navigate the institution and rules, while left entirely to their own initiative. College courses and their degree of difficulty can range from an emphasis on breadth over depth to a demand for critical thinking and rigorous analysis. Mostly, the curriculum forces students to take copious notes and prove they can memorize the information that's been prioritized by the institution with a limited allowance for critical thinking.

There's a high level of stress that comes with having to memorize information for upcoming tests. Students end up constantly checking their grades, their class rankings, and stressing about their GPA, when right after the test is over they can't remember half of what they were "taught." Standardized tests contribute to this mix of anxiety and unproductive learning habits.

Moreover, all these pressure-based educational measures can

create unprofitable attitudes in students. They care far more about how many points an assignment is worth or knowing what format the test will be (let's all remind ourselves that multiple choice tests don't exist in real life!) instead of focusing their attention on the material.

Many will spend more time figuring out how to hack the system, such as finding CliffsNotes or using Google Translate, than learning new skills or producing original work. Research Professor of Psychology Peter Gray talks about this epidemic in his TEDTalk entitled "How Our Schools Thwart Passions."[25] He has studied how the increased focus on college admissions in high school has added excessive stress to students, while at the same time diluting creative thinking and problem-solving.

The Hazard of Self-Sabotaging Behavior

Free of parental supervision and discovering that the university provides few, if any, restraints on bad behavior, most students find themselves unprepared to discipline their own conduct. I witnessed a lot of self-sabotaging behavior, including heavy drinking, preoccupation with Greek Social life, and unrelenting dating pursuits.

That said, I'd say the biggest culprits of my college challenges were my tendency to procrastinate and my general flakiness, which I deeply regret. As the semester progressed, I lost control over the homework and the cataloging of the firehose of information I was trying to input. I slacked off in class, and although I always attended, I wasn't really engaged. I resorted to pulling all-nighters to complete projects and prepare for tests, which resulted in failing to really understand what was being taught and finding myself dozing off in class.

In his article, "Professors Reveal the Craziest Things Students Have Done During Class," Peter Jacobs shares an account from a teaching assistant, the episode of the dressed-up taco taking a math test:[26]

> I was a TA for a calculus class a few years ago. With just under 10 minutes to go in a 50-minute midterm exam, a student bursts into the classroom dressed in a taco costume, sweating, completely out of breath, grabs a test from the front desk and starts to frantically write. At first, I thought it was some prank and I tried to kick him out. Turns out he was enrolled in the class and apparently just passed out at a Halloween party the night before and woke up with no time to change clothes. I let him take the test in the remaining 7 or so minutes.

Again, wise words from Jung sum up the hazard here: "I have always been impressed by the fact that there are a surprising number of individuals who never use their minds if they can avoid it, and an equal number who do use their minds, but in an amazingly stupid way."

Surviving the Curve of Cultural Adaptation

Every college student is going to experience, probably for the first time, the curve of cultural adaptation. This curve typically refers to people moving into a foreign country.

When you move to a new country or a region that is quite different from what you're used to, you'll undergo exposure to the curve of cultural adaptation, which can best be explained by this simple graph:[27]

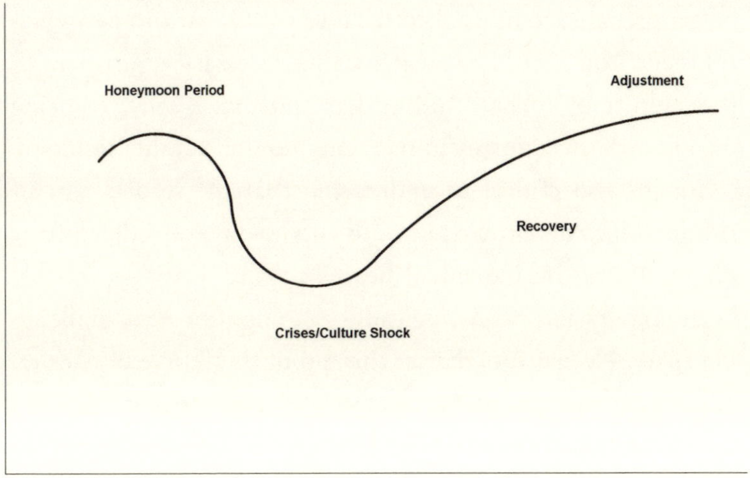

Notice that the experience begins well enough with a "honeymoon" phase, where all seems wonderful. But that is soon followed by the depths of a crisis or "culture shock" as an individual comes face-to-face with having to adapt to all the differences of a new environment.

Unfortunately, no one ever brings up this concept with college students. It's understandably a huge change for foreign students traveling to the United States for schooling, but college also represents a major adjustment for all students entering the new and unfamiliar world of higher education. College, the college campus, and college life are all substantially different from the previous experiences of the majority of new students. That's one of the reasons colleges offer orientations for incoming students.

But the orientation sessions alone may not prepare you for the gut-punch of this particular learning curve.

If you know ahead of time to anticipate this learning curve and its attendant social and emotional discomfort, you're much better prepared to move through it as you adjust to a new environment. You should be aware of this necessary adjustment to the "culture of college" and understand that a sense of being off-kilter can accompany immersion into this new life situation.

But it's also critical to understand that the second part of this learning curve trends upward and involves an "adjustment" phase, where the individual begins to find a way—probably both literally and psychologically—through the new, challenging space. Notice, too, that at the end of this "curve of cultural adaptation" process, there is recovery! People can and do regain their emotional balance and even discover a sense of belonging in their new environment.

Even if you are feeling some anxiety about the path ahead, that's perfectly normal. Almost everybody experiences some combination of excitement and anxiety when starting something new, particularly when the new thing is as life-altering as college. But the nerves will subside, and you can have a wonderful experience as you step into your new life.

Katherine, a college freshman, tells her story as she reflects on her first-year experience:[28]

> I was overcome by a multitude of conflicting emotions as I was about to begin this new chapter in my life. As I walked into my dorm room, I was immediately greeted with an embrace from my roommate; this comforting act erased all my fears and unanswered questions about this

new home of mine.

This year has been an adventure I had never experienced. I thought with all the freedom and independence, it would negatively affect me and my maturity level, but the opposite happened. Being alone in an unfamiliar setting forced me to go outside my comfort zone. Not only did I learn how to rely on individuals I wasn't fully comfortable around, but I also had to understand the importance of independence and making my own decisions without any outside insight. It's okay to be scared and a little bit terrified in making this unfamiliar place your new home. Not only have I learned from my own first-year experience, but also by doing this project, college will quickly become the best and most comforting home you've ever had. The people will become your siblings, you'll find your favorite meal which you get excited to see on the cafeteria menu, you'll discover your favorite spot on campus to do homework. You'll discover so much about yourself, some things that you'd never even consider yourself capable of. Looking at myself now, I've changed in ways that I never would have guessed at the beginning of the year. College has helped pull me out of my comfort zone, engage in sometimes controversial discussions, and grow as an individual. I've learned so many life lessons just throughout my first year here, and after interviewing some of my classmates, I know that I'm not alone.

Katherine experienced the normal nervousness that accompanies entering the new environment of college, but she also successfully navigated her adjustment to this new situation. Furthermore, she was clearly able to identify and gather a posse around herself of people she'd never met before, but whom she now refers to as "siblings." That's a major transformation that you, too, will have the opportunity to experience!

The significance is that this adjustment is natural to every new student. Just because none of your classmates mention it or put a name on it doesn't mean you're the only one going through it. It's a common experience that has been chronicled and charted.

You will find that the feelings and fears associated with transition recur often in your life as you move into adulthood, get your first important job, or make a major relocation to maximize your job opportunities. New environments demand this type of adjustment, and it always takes energy. But if you know that there is a typical cycle that everyone experiences, and that it repeats whenever you enter a brand-new environment or "culture," then you will be more likely to see this experience as less stressful, knowing you're moving toward the recovery phase at the end. I hope that will be the case for you.

There's Hope Ahead

College beckons to us, for it offers the chance to live on our own, find new friends, explore interesting ideas, and facilitate our transition into adulthood. But it's an uncertain road. I'm sure new students and their parents are craning for a glimpse further down that unchartered path. This means college is bound to be stressful. College students find themselves suddenly separated from their traditional support system of family and friends while facing new challenges, such as living with roommates, managing heavy workloads, and developing an independent identity. It's no surprise that anxiety often spikes during college.

Those feelings of apprehension and anxiety are shared by virtually every student that takes the first step into higher education. Your college selection can advance your education and understanding of the world, but also assist you in making a number of transitions during this time of change and growth. When you've chosen well, your college can provide a new environment in which you can soon experience a sense of belonging.

Our Inherently Flawed Perspective

Even if we choose not to goof off and engage in self-sabotaging behavior in college, and we know about the curve of cultural adaptation, we still need to be aware of the hidden hazard inherent in just being a human. The problem is, we just don't know what we don't know, especially about ourselves. We each have our own unique perspectives. Yet some of our perspectives are inherently flawed, misconceived, or flat-out wrong; these hinder our ability to learn and to connect with people.

Here's an interesting illustration of our inherently flawed perspective. If you ask most people what they see when they close their eyes, they will say "black." However, the color which we can see when we close our eyes is actually called *eigengrau* (a German word, meaning eye gray) which is different from black! So even when we close our eyes, we fail to see the truth. It sounds like a little detail but it's essential in the many things that are conveyed in our observation of the world around us.

How do we correct for our unperceived errors when we don't always have clarity about what we're actually seeing? One way is to make sure we elicit other perspectives to inform our own views. College, if properly exploited, can provide an opportunity for this type of self-discovery, putting you in a position to relate to other people and ideas, gain differing perspectives, and build a broader awareness of the world that can give you an edge in navigating life.

Similarly, there's a well-known psychological phenomenon that also skews our view. It's called the fundamental attribution bias, which says that people are more likely to blame someone else's failings on that person's personality trait, while they chalk their own shortcomings up to situational circumstances.[29] Given such inherent tendencies at play, it's difficult for anyone to be truly accurate and objective when it comes to assessing personality traits—even their own. If you're aware of this phenomenon, however, you can use it to your advantage. As Jung put it, "Everything that irritates us about others can lead to an understanding of ourselves."

This is why you should connect with your class cohorts to engage in discussion and share concerns. It's a powerful way to see more clearly, avoid the hazard of fundamental attribution bias, and learn valuable information about yourself and the world around you. It does involve leaving your comfort zone. It means starting a conversation (yes, face-to-face) with someone you've seen but not heard. Then you try it again with someone else. We'll discuss more about the necessity and value of creating those connections in the next section.

PART III

Companions Along the Path

THERE'S A WELL-KNOWN AFRICAN PROVERB that says, "If you want to go fast, go alone; if you want to go far, go together." There's a lot of wisdom in that notion. As this proverb points out, walking the path with others is imperative for the long haul ahead.

While it may seem an attractive option to "go it alone," unencumbered by the demands of learning to relate to others along the way, the impulse toward that kind of misguided individualism can keep you from success in the long run.

In this section, I'll share with you some insights on how to resist the urge to isolate. I'll explain why you should gather and nurture a core group of people—your posse—who can walk along with you and offer mutual support and companionship through college. We'll then discuss how to expand those relationships into a much larger community, a network of contacts that can sustain and encourage your personal and professional development far beyond your college years.

CHAPTER 5

Gathering Your Posse

"There are good ships and wood ships, ships that sail the sea, but the best ships are friendships, may they always be!"

– IRISH PROVERB

Fostering Student Connectedness and Building Relationships

The relationships you forge in college can and will be a lifeline for you throughout your life and career. Learning how to collaborate with fellow classmates is as important as developing credentials and expertise. Forging relationships during college enhances the value of academic achievement; while study groups contribute to academic performance, relationships that survive graduation will have a profound impact on your life, equal to or even greater than any scholastic accomplishments.

In fact, building relationships is one of the best ways to continuously develop. Making introductions and expanding your network of relationships can help develop new ideas and ways of thinking, share experiences and intelligence, find sources of support, develop skills, and increase awareness—just to name a few advantages. It can even facilitate self-discovery.

I call this process "gathering your posse." In classic movies of the Wild West, a posse was the group of citizens a sheriff would recruit to help bring outlaws to justice; the posse would help find the bad guys, and they'd always have the sheriff's back if there was any trouble. The word comes from medieval Latin, where *posse* means "be able," while the Anglo-Normans altered the same root to make "power." Now the term is used more loosely to describe any group of friends who share common interests and look out for one another, but the core idea is the same: it's easier to move forward if you're surrounded by similarly motivated people. Your posse is the friends you make in college who will travel the trail with you, a trustworthy band who offer good company, a measure of safety, extra power, and the potential of great capability in college and beyond.

College offers access to an educated, motivated peer group. It offers students a community of peers who share interests and aspirations; a collegiate community that gives testimony to the power of being a member of a cohort and the support that can come with it. Whether it's forming study groups or participating in collaborative projects, how you work with fellow students can be a powerful influence on the quality of your college experience. But you need to learn how to "play nice" with cohort members and learn from the power of shared college experiences.

I attended a college with about 4,000 undergraduates, and I was amazed at how many students I got to know either by name or just by facial recognition. There are many venues that offer the opportunity to meet fellow students. The dormitory is one place. The classroom offers the chance to get acquainted with students in more formal academic setting, in which we find ourselves working collaboratively with fellow students. These may be students you wouldn't ordinarily run into. In four years, I got to know several hundred fellow classmates. The tragedy is that I left just as I arrived—just one person, without a posse. I hope that will not be your experience.

The Power of the Posse

We've all read or heard about the book *Lord of the Flies*, a dismal tale of what happens when a group of boys get stranded on a desert island, and how they descend into tribalism and cruelty, losing all connection to civilization and the society from which they came. A rescuing naval officer's comment says it all: "I should have thought that a pack of British boys would have put on a better show than that?"

The novel was written by William Golding and is one of the most widely read works of fiction written since World War II. It's been interpreted politically, religiously, anthropologically, and psychologically although the story is quite simple. The book goes into detailed descriptions of how kids descend into primitive tribalism, committing acts of uncivilized degradation and supreme cruelty. The premise of the book was civilization is only a thin veneer barely preventing people from reverting to primitive behavior.

The book substantially influenced society, and the recurring rioting and looting that we have witnessed serves as a reminder of just how easily people can descend into uncivilized behavior.

Golding's dystopian views were not only influenced by witnessing first-hand the brutality of war, but also by long observations from when he worked at an English boys' school. Golding was a troubled soul, an admitted child bully who had contempt for his students and often reeled against the stultifying class system of postwar Britain.

Lord of the Flies was intended as an allegory, and the island was meant to be a microcosm of the world. It says more perhaps about Golding's despair than the world itself, and for decades, writers have been searching for a brighter take on humanity.[30]

They found an account of a real-life castaway incident in 1965 described in the Guardian newspaper.[31] The account is based on excerpts taken from Rutger Bregman's book *Humankind* and on news reports and actual interviews with one of the boys, as well as with the captain who rescued them.

Contrary to the gruesome story of tribalism portrayed in *Lord of the Flies*, the real story of what happened is a surprising example of how a posse formed and functioned well. The largely unnoticed real adventure started in Tonga in 1965, Bregman writes. Six boys between the ages of 13 and 16 decided to skip school and sail from Tonga to Fiji on a "borrowed" fisherman's boat. They stocked the boat with food and supplies but fell asleep on their first night at sea. When they awoke, their boat had been damaged by the waves and was left adrift for days. Finally, the boys washed up on a rocky, uninhabited island, where they managed to survive for over a year.

Australian Captain Peter Warner ultimately found the boys after spotting a fire while sailing near the island in 1966. Warner told Bregman of his shock at seeing a naked, long-haired child that came up on shore to greet him. "My name is Stephen," the boy said, according to Bregman's story. "There are six of us here and we reckon we've been here 15 months."

Rather than descend into tribal warfare over limited resources, the boys had managed to put together a good life on their remote island. "The boys had set up a small commune with a food garden, hollowed-out tree trunks to store rainwater, a gymnasium with curious weights, a badminton court, chicken pens, and a permanent fire," Warner wrote in his memoirs.

The boys had even crafted a homemade guitar made from driftwood and coconut shells. They survived the early days of their ordeal by eating fish, coconuts, and birds, but their lives got better when they eventually climbed to the top of a rocky cliff on the island, where they discovered the remains of an abandoned settlement around a volcanic crater, as well as seeds, bananas, and chickens that had descended from the former inhabitants' farms.

The schoolboys said they got through the ordeal by laying out a few ground rules. They worked in pairs, issued time-outs to avoid fights, and held regular song and prayer sessions at the beginning and end of each day. I think this real-life event underscores the schoolboys' ability to work together in a supportive posse and how that allowed them to survive and even flourish on their own as a group for over a year.

The college experience may not be as extreme as the one faced by those stranded boys, but college provides an opportunity to collect a similar, supportive posse that can thrive when its members learn to cooperate in highly stressful situations.

The Distinction Between a Tribe and a Posse

What the author of *Lord of the Flies* offered up is a fictional tribal perspective, based on his imaginative views on primitive man who survived through the formation of clans of hunters and foragers. Primitive man existed on the edge of survival in a harsh environment; to survive required a hierarchical structure that was just as harsh. To this day, we humans retain many of those instinctive behaviors and thinking patterns, even though our environment has changed for the better. Thus, it's in our nature to form clans or tribes. From the Ice Age on, forming a tribe was a way to improve the odds of survival. As we've gotten more sophisticated, it's become a way to increase our chances of success. There are a lot of positive outcomes associated with tribes: they can help us generate a more reliable food supply, provide shelter, develop specialized trades, and live healthier lives.

Nowadays, there are all sorts of tribes, some are subtle while others are less so. In an office environment, although everyone works for the same company, there likely exist several tribes, separated by profession, personality type, and background. Take, for example, the most common of opposing tribes, salespeople versus engineers. Their roles are about as opposite as two groups can be. One group is composed of extroverts while the other is composed of introverts. They can and may harbor a level of disdain for each other, but nevertheless, they have to work together in order for the company, their employer, to thrive.

How do you get aggressive, fast-talking salespeople to cooperate with reserved, detail-oriented engineers? What enables intuitive, creative types to sync with budget-minded planners? Even though they are part of the same organization, their loyalty usually belongs to their smaller, more intimate tribe. In a corporate environment, that tribe is usually composed of 20 to 150 people. It forms naturally, even inside an elaborate, highly structured corporation and has a special staying power. Even if a member of the tribe leaves a company, you'll probably keep in touch, just because of your shared history and common bond. A tribe exists because it's often composed of people with shared values. The problem with belonging to a tribe is that it often comes at the expense of losing a part of yourself and suborning your identity.

By contrast, choosing to develop a posse offers you the chance to find and define yourself in relation to a supportive and cooperative group. While tribes can be largely hierarchal, exclusive, and even gender specific, an academic posse tends to be a flat hierarchy, equal in structure, with each member contributing in their own unique way, and they're often co-ed. Because all team members are included and valued, you never know from which posse member a special insight may originate.

The Power of Your Cohort

In college, you can build relationships with your cohort classmates to form posse study groups, social groups, or drinking companions. Any extracurricular activities in which members share a passion can also be the basis for forming relationships.

Typically, college students represent a skewed group, composed of highly intelligent, competitive individuals who are there for a purpose. College brings together people who would never have crossed paths on their own. It allows you to belong to a group without losing yourself. And it offers you access to like-minded people of a similar age who will make up your community for the next four years. You're given the opportunity to get to know a slice of the cohort you belong to and network and collaborate within this community.

Being effective at building your posse, however, means emphasizing collaboration and not competitive behavior in dealing with fellow classmates. When we're young, our instincts are to compete with those around us, but that's a mistake. What often gets in the way of building relationships is petty competitiveness and juvenile behavior. Even a silly slight can be an excuse for disdain or even to "ghost" someone. An emotionally mature person doesn't succumb to such petty, partisan behavior. It's better to embrace emotional maturity and act collaboratively.

Your Cohort Is Unique

Belonging to a cohort and finding ways to work together productively should be one of your highest priorities. College cohorts offer access to group intelligence and provide hacks to everyday student life.

The concept of shared generational behavior can be used to locate particular birth cohorts in specific historical and cultural circumstances. They possess shared psychological and sociological dimensions that create a sense of belonging and identity, which may define a generation or a cohort ranging over a decade or more in birth dates. Technology has had an impact on social behavior and shifted values. The difference from one generation to the next is becoming increasingly defined. The one thing that you can be assured of is that both the public and private sector will embrace your cohort, and that your cohort will become the center of attention for industry, markets, and demographic specialists.

Historically, generations were referred to in family relationship terms without giving effect to social or societal changes. But technology, starting with the industrial age, has had an enormous impact on succeeding generations in terms of group behavior and convention. The concept is that generations can be imprinted by specific historical events that cause young people to perceive the world differently than their elders.

Historian Hans Jaeger proved the impact of thought coalesced in describing how generations form. According to the pulse-rate hypothesis, a society's entire population can be divided into a series of non-overlapping cohorts, each of which develops a unique "peer personality" because of the time that each cohort came of age.[32]

Effectively, generations and their behaviors are formed by specific historical events that cause young people to perceive the world differently than their elders. Thus, not everyone may be part of a generation; only those who share a unique social and biographical experience of an important historical moment are recognized as a defined generation.

While all generations have similarities, there are differences among them as well. A 2010 Pew Research Center report called "Millennials: Confident. Connected. Open to Change." noted the challenge of studying generations:[33]

> Generational analysis has a long and distinguished place in social science, and so behavioral scholars believe it is not only possible, but often highly illuminating, to search for the unique and distinctive characteristics of any given age

> group of Americans. But we also know this is not an exact science. We are mindful that there are as many differences in attitudes, values, behaviors, and lifestyles within a generation as there are between generations. But we believe this reality does not diminish the value of generational analysis; it merely adds to its richness and complexity.

Self-Discovery within a Cohort

The need to define our own identity is universal. Interacting with classmates will help you frame your identity. A cohort offers a place for personal discovery by providing a venue for comparing oneself to others. That comparison can produce a more objective view of ourselves, our skills, and our competitive standing.

Do you have the stuff it takes to rise in the grade ranking of your class? It takes more than attending class and preparing for tests; it takes going beyond the day-to-day demands of the class and conducting extra research on the subject being taught. It requires special talent that may answer the question of whether we are born with confidence or gain it. When offered the opportunity to better yourself, you must work for it and not just wish and dream. The formation of study groups can act as a catalyst for forging your knowledge and understanding of the academic studies you must complete to gain your degree. The whole experience of being part of a network of motivated individuals will likely prove to be as much of an asset as the academic skills and knowledge you acquire in college.

Even the best of us watches the clock during class, counting down the time until we get a break. But don't miss out on the value of that time. Classrooms offer you the opportunity to draw comparisons and measure yourself against other classmates. The class is an arena in which students are measured by the same standards, providing a relative comparison of skills, aptitude, and intelligence. You get to know your classmates. You get to take full measure of fellow students in skills, intelligence, and depth of understanding, which can provide a relative comparison to yourself.

What Is Friendship, Really?

When choosing companions for your journey, it's important to think carefully about friendships, acquaintances, and networks and how these groups overlap and differ. What you should cultivate is access to a diversity of opinions and healthy arguments. You gain perspective by soaking up knowledge and by exposing yourself to contrasting perspectives. People are different. Things that make you happy might not make another person happy. Your idea of support might differ from the next person's. The key is finding people that are good for you and learning to recognize who is good for you as you start to get acquainted.

Hopefully, you can find people that will inspire you to be a better person, motivate you to achieve your goals, empower you to make the changes you need to succeed, and cheer your success. That's hard to accomplish in real life, not least because it requires a mutual aspect. I was never able to assemble such a group. I may have had that kind of interaction with a select number of people over abbreviated moments in time, but never on a long-term, well-defined basis.

One reason gathering a reliable posse is hard is because it's human nature to take for granted those close to us. Friendships require an enormous investment of time, patience, and intimacy. It's hard to balance these friendships and maintain an equilibrium. As one friendship grows and becomes more intimate, it may crowd out an earlier friendship. Consequently, friendships are very hard to sustain.

You may find yourself developing an online friendship, but as that grows, an in-person relationship may wane. We expect way too much from friendship. We all have beefs with friends and acquaintances. But it's amazing how many friends and family may have a beef with us.

Further, most of us don't distinguish between friends and acquaintances; in fact, most of us have few friends. It's a challenge to maintain friendships. There are many levels of friendship, from casual ones based on shared circumstances, to those based on a shared interest, or relationships based on confidence-sharing. True friends can be a source of support and validation. Does this person lift you up? Are they happy about your success? Do they cheer for you? Do they care enough to push you or ask uncomfortable questions when you're off track?

Think about this: a study conducted at the Massachusetts Institute of Technology (MIT) suggested that true friendship might be an illusion. An MIT poll of friends found that only half of those we think of as friends actually like us, and only a third of friendships are mutual.[34]

One explanation is that we simply assume our feelings are shared—that's because the thought that the people we value don't feel the same about us would be too unsettling and hurtful. Again, we have this tendency to project onto other people a certain set of sensibilities without proper justification or fact-based affirmation. It's also possible that many unreciprocated friendships are aspirational, with people naming popular or powerful individuals as friends, even when they don't know them very well. The popular person, in contrast, has lots of "friends" to choose from, so they can afford to be pickier, experts say.

The rise of social media has blurred the definition of friendship. Ronald Sharp, professor of English at Vassar College, says: "People are so eager to maximize the efficiency of relationships that they have lost touch with what it is to be a friend."

While many of the people you meet will remain acquaintances, some of them may become your friends. But often, the difference between friends and acquaintances is dependent, in part, on how much you want to expose yourself to others. Plus, which sides of yourself you're willing to reveal will also have an impact. Alternatively, not everyone is going to like you. No matter what you do, you'll never be accepted by certain people, and that's just the way it is.

There's a fine line between exposing one's vulnerable self and coming across as needy and insecure. Once you see the soft, mushy side of a person, that person tends to become a lot less interesting. A true friend is someone who cares so much, they will risk offending you by having that uncomfortable conversation to let you know when you're on a destructive path or undermining yourself. A true friend wants what's in your best interest. However, that kind of thinking puts a lot of burden on friendship. I'm not sure that most prospective friends are willing to assume that degree of burden.

The path to friendship is a relationship in which both parties have equal standing. It fosters mutual respect, which allows two people to withstand stress and disagreement. There has to be an element of reciprocity. But all of those factors are hard to achieve with a broad number of individuals, and that's the beauty of networking and building acquaintances. The basis for these relationships is nowhere near as demanding, but still can be very rewarding.

Your Posse Will Have Your Back

"The future ain't what it used to be," according to legendary Yankees catcher and manager, Yogi Berra, famous for his hilarious and truth-revealing "Berra-isms." His statement seems almost prophetic now, as we imagine just how different the future might be than we ever anticipated in the past. The cycle of progress is accelerating. The changes that we will experience in the next ten years will likely be greater than the changes experienced over the last 100 years. We stand on the brink of a technological revolution that will fundamentally alter the way we live, work, and relate to one another. In its scale, scope, and complexity, the transformation will be unlike anything humankind has experienced before. We do not yet know just how it will unfold, but one thing is clear: the response to it must be integrated and comprehensive, involving all stakeholders of the global polity, from the public and private sectors to academia and civil society. The key to adjusting well with this change is a posse that will have your back.

The First Industrial Revolution used water and steam power to mechanize production. The Second used electric power to create mass production. The Third used electronics and information technology to automate production. Now a Fourth Industrial Revolution is building on the Third—a digital revolution that has been occurring since the middle of the last century.[35] It's characterized by a fusion of technologies that is blurring the lines between the physical, digital, and biological spheres. The speed of current breakthroughs has no historical precedent. When compared with previous industrial revolutions, the Fourth is evolving at an exponential rather than a linear pace. Moreover, it is disrupting almost every industry in every country. And the breadth and depth of these changes herald the transformation of entire systems of production, management, and governance.

The possibilities created by billions of people being connected by mobile devices, with unprecedented processing power, storage capacity, and access to knowledge, are unlimited. And these possibilities will be multiplied by emerging technology breakthroughs in fields such as artificial intelligence (AI), robotics, the Internet of Things, autonomous vehicles, 3D printing, nanotechnology, biotechnology, materials science, energy storage, and quantum computing. Already artificial intelligence is all around us, from self-driving cars and drones to virtual assistants and software that translate or invest.

The Fourth Industrial Revolution is a fusion of advances in all of these things. This perfect storm of technologies is paving the way for transforming how we live and radically disrupting almost every business sector. And it's all happening at an unprecedented, whirlwind pace.

While you have no control over the pace of coming changes, you can prepare for traveling into the uncertain future by developing and maintaining your posse. Research has shown the formation of distinctive cohorts based on date range in births over the last 75 years. We have witnessed profound changes in the behavior of different cohorts. Millennials, the generation born between 1981 and 1999, behave differently from Baby Boomers, born between 1948 and 1964, and Generation X, born between 1965 and 1980. Even more recently, the cycles of progress and obsolescence have accelerated significantly, and the technology that has come about in the last 20 years has shaped human behavior, resulting in each subsequent generation adopting unique behavior not shared by previous generations. Businesses have picked up on these demographic developments. To survive the changing trends in human behavior, they have to adopt demography in promoting their products. Your ability to play nice within your cohort will be a factor in your career development.

Belonging to a specific demographic cohort is both advantageous and disadvantageous. We talked about the advantages, but one disadvantage is that as you age your cohort will be displaced by succeeding cohorts who are destined to become the next center of attention for markets, products, and services. The progression of technology will also increase discrimination between emerging cohorts and aging cohorts.

Steve Jobs' quote below acknowledges this hard truth of life and gives recognition to the inevitable aging and displacement of cohorts:[36]

> No one wants to die. Even people who want to go to heaven don't want to die to get there. And yet death is the destination we all share. No one has ever escaped it. And that is as it should be, because Death is very likely the single best invention of Life. It is Life's change agent. It clears out the old to make way for the new. Right now, the new is you,

> but someday not too long from now, you will gradually become the old and be cleared away.
>
> Sorry to be so dramatic, but it is quite true.

Further, with the rapid changes taking place and their pronounced impact on human behavior, your career will likely be heavily buffeted by these changes, and the posse that you have garnered from your college experience could be the source of your lifeline. These are the people who will have your back in challenging times.

Moreover, there is a good chance that your posse will help you to maintain your competitive edge. They can provide you with valuable intelligence on coming trends and industry changes, the formation of new business models, and the impact of disruptive technology.

Breaking through Resistance to Build Relationships

For some of us, cultivating the relationships that will form our posse can be a real challenge, and introverts among us may find this particularly intimidating. It can be very tempting to go it alone, especially because developing and maintaining relationships does involve skill and work. But human beings are capable of learning to make social adjustments, even in difficult circumstances.

Consider what it must be like serving on a nuclear submarine.[37] The typical nuclear sub is a little over the length of a football field but only 40 feet wide. The crew is composed of 110 men and women who must share two showers, four toilets, and one urinal. Crew members must share bunks. About a third of the crew is asleep at any given moment during the 24-hour day. They work in shifts, normally six hours on, 12 hours off. Only the captain and executive officer of the submarine have private rooms in which they work and sleep. Given the limited number of bunks, the service members must hot bunk. That means when one person gets up, another takes over that bunk. Most of the crew are engineering introverts. We know this because service on submarines requires the most intensive qualification and training of any specialty military service. If they can learn to live in close quarters for months at a time, you as a college student can develop the social skills required to network and build relationships with your fellow classmates in an area covering several hundred acres of campus space.

Lasting College Relationships

College relationships can be extraordinary; in fact, they can last a lifetime. These relationships can be extremely durable, surviving breakups, geographical distances, and long periods of absence. The fact is that friendships—even those that have lasted a long time—can and will fizzle out. People change over time. Their interests and perspectives evolve. But college relationships have an advantage, since they are often the outcome of an academic forging process that includes shared stress, shared discovery, and close quarter exposure. This, combined with the sense of nostalgia that only builds over time, can result in the formation of some of the most durable relationships. This shared nostalgia will allow you to reconnect with almost any classmate, no matter how much time has transpired.

The college environment, which puts a large number of peers together in close quarters, is an ideal setting for forging long-lasting friendships. You and your classmates share a common thread that inspired you to elect to attend college, generally, and that college, particularly. Plus, you're all going through the same transition into adulthood in the midst of academic challenges and anxiety.

Working in close quarters invariably strips away all pretenses. The irony is that the best way to form friendships is not by demonstrating one's academic achievement or athletic prowess, but rather by exposing your vulnerable side. You risk alienating people by overshadowing them and making them feel inadequate. Alternatively, classroom sessions offer many opportunities to either make a fool of oneself or to fall short of academic achievement. Who hasn't experienced that humiliating moment when you're called upon by a professor and caught flat-footed, stumbling over your words in a desperate search for an answer that will placate your instructor? Presenting your vulnerable side in the classroom may not necessarily be a disaster. A lot of people can relate to the person who came up short that day. Consequently, classrooms offer an opportunity for accidental friendships and fortuitous alliances that can never be replicated in your personal life or post graduate life. I would contend that as one gets older it becomes increasingly difficult to forge new friendships. This is why college is so important when it comes to developing lasting relationships.

Once you've selected and gathered your college posse, you're in a wonderful position to build and expand those relationships into a larger network of supportive contacts that you can retain as you move forward into your life and career after college. Most people don't have the foresight to get a jump on this relational effort in college, but if you can start early, you'll be setting yourself up for success down the road. We'll look at some ways to do that in the next chapter.

CHAPTER 6

The Company You Keep

"No man is an island entire of itself; every man is a piece of the continent, a part of the main."
– JOHN DONNE

No One Is an Island

To me, these lines from John Donne's poem evoke a sense of community, not the one we build with friends and family, but one that reflects the fact that we're all connected by belonging to a larger, global community. The poem recognizes that we're all in this endeavor, traversing life's struggles, facing its consequences together, and that forms the basis for why we should work to establish and maintain connections with one another. More inclusively stated, we can acknowledge that, indeed, no person is an island because we're all part of something greater than ourselves.

Remember that you're not an island, even if you sometimes feel isolated in the challenges you face. You're part of a human connectedness, and as a member of a cohort, you can use the power of that connection to survive and thrive!

So Who Do You Know?

There's wisdom in the maxim that it's not *what* you know, it's *who* you know. It's the antithesis to what college education represents, with its focus on course content and skill acquisition; that is to say, *what* you know.[38]

Instead embrace the "who you know" philosophy now, instead of continuing to play it safe while setting yourself up for regrets about what could have been. Meet new people. Get to know who they are, what they do, and where they come from. Learn about their goals, dreams, and willingness to share in friendship, or at least association. Consider this an investment in human capital from the perspective of building long-term connections. As you go through college with your selected posse, plan to keep these people with you along the way, and then begin to create an ever-expanding network of supportive people as you move into your career.

What Do I Mean by Networking?

Typically, whenever someone mentions networking, what comes to mind is attending a job fair or a college-sponsored corporate visit. These are artificial exercises where you get all dressed up and put your game face on to bravely engage in dialogue with perfect strangers. In such situations, the interviewer has all the power, while you are trying to be appealing as you subject yourself to scrutiny. This is clearly *not* what I'm referring to. Rather, college offers the ideal laboratory for developing and building relationships with classmates, upperclassmen, professors, alumni, and college guidance and psychological counselors. You'll want to get to know people in all of these categories, for they may one day be your best resource.

In the age of Facebook, Twitter, Instagram, and all the rest, you're already familiar with social networks. You gain followers on Instagram and add friends on Snapchat. Networking, in the professional sense, is similar but you're establishing connections with people who share certain objectives in life. These connections could be students in other majors, class leaders, college alumni, or even professors. The purpose of networking is to form relationships with people who have ambition, understanding, and awareness that may help you get to where you want to go, and the earlier you start building up your network, the better. That's why it's important to start networking in college, well before you're ready to enter the workforce.

Art of Networking

As a prospective college student, networking is far from a pressing concern for you right now. You may just be trying to get through another public speaking class without throwing up or pass your accounting exam without forgetting how to do the math. But trust me, the future you, who may be happily employed, will thank the present you for building a professional network now.

There's an art to networking. Be careful not to pre-judge the people you meet. Some of your classmates may appear to be idiots, but after graduation who knows where they may land.

You don't want to be discriminating with whom you are friendly or build a relationship. One day they just might work at your dream company, and you can say, "Hey, remember me from the college class?" Make networking an everyday routine by engaging with professors and classmates.

Consequential Strangers

The story below, from a *New York Times* column by David Brooks in 2018, demonstrates the importance of friendship and consequential relations.[39]

> Bob Hall was a rancher. In 1936, in the depths of the Depression, he was suffering from a cancer that was eating the flesh on the side of his face. His ranch had dwindled to nearly nothing, and weeks after bankers took the last of his livestock, Hall died, leaving his family deeply in debt.
>
> His sons pleaded with anybody they could find to give them a loan and save the family ranch. No one would do it. Finally, in desperation, they went to their neighbor, Buzz Newton—who was known for his miserliness—and asked him to co-sign a loan. "I always thought so much of your dad; he was the most generous man I have known," Newton answered. "Yes, I'll co-sign the note."
>
> Bob Hall's grandson, also named Robert Hall, drew out the lesson in his book "This Land of Strangers," noting: "The truth is, relationships are the most valuable and value-creating resource of any society. They are our lifelines to survive, grow and thrive."

You can never predict when someone you know, even casually, may turn out to be the very person who will step in to help when you most need it.

Horizontal Networking—Meeting Your Posse on the Path

We've discussed the power of gathering your supportive posse to help you in college. But consider this: college is the best time to hone one of your most powerful career-building tools—networking with those who are already walking with you on the same path. Start networking with your posse! Unfortunately, you won't hear much about the importance of networking in your college classes—and it's not because you're daydreaming during the lecture. It's just that professional networking doesn't really fit into a typical chemistry syllabus or world literature discussion.

The good news is there are lots of ways to make connections happen. Start with getting involved on campus through a myriad ways, including honor societies, professional clubs, social sororities and fraternities, campus jobs, student media, and student clubs. In such circumstances, not only will you be able to connect with other students, but you may also have opportunities to connect with speakers, advisers, and mentors.

If your campus has an involvement or club fair, go! Or sign up for a campus email newsletter, peruse the bulletin boards in the study lounges or library, and talk to classmates and friends. As cheesy as it sounds, there's something out there for everyone.

Spend some time at the campus career center, which provides valuable, free resources. The center offers access to career guidance counselors. It can also offer access to psychologists and personality and aptitude testing that can help you gain better insights about your talents and true interests.

The main point is to reach out beyond your regular clique to forge new personal and professional connections. Don't play it safe—those added relationships will strengthen your peer-support group and help fast-track your way to quicker and greater career success.

Handling Rejection

Making new friends, especially ones for life, is risky. There's always the chance of rejection, hurt feelings, embarrassment, or worse yet, being abandoned by your existing circle of friends who lack curiosity and understanding to let newcomers into their world.

Maybe you feel too shy and introverted to reach out when a new kid, classmate, or associate moves into the neighborhood, for example. Maybe you just lack the confidence or know-how to network. To make connections work for you, as well as for the other person, it ultimately needs to be of mutual benefit.

Here's the thing: new acquaintances and those of lesser acquaintance are more likely to be connected to other, more-distinguishing networks of people than your close friends. Such people can serve as social bridges to novel worlds that are relatively unknown to us. They might expand our world in unexpected and serendipitous ways. It's a shame to waste or miss such opportunities. I call it the power of weak personal bonds. An acquaintance based on similar interests is more likely to generate a meaningful lead than one that may arise from our close friendships.

Don't live a life of regret, in which you deny yourself opportunities to make new connections. Doing so will only set you up for disappointment later in life. Don't put yourself in the position of wishing you could have a do-over—once you have acquired the maturity and moxie to know how and when to stretch yourself and enlarge your circle of friends and mentors. Make it happen now.

We all have our own unique perspectives. The problem is that some of our perspectives are inherently flawed, misconceived, or flat-out wrong, and these hinder our ability to connect with people. Sometimes, you just have to fight your way past that stuff. Again, it's about getting out of your comfort zone. Start a conversation (yes, face-to-face) with someone you've seen but not heard. Then try it again with someone else. Turn it into a game, a competition with yourself. Be ready for new opportunities as you grow your circle of connections. Welcome to networking!

Vertical Networking—the Power of Nostalgia

While networking among your classmates and gathering a posse can best be characterized as horizontal in nature, another form of networking is vertical networking, forging relations with college professors, education counselors, placement counselors, and college alumni. It has to do with leveraging the power of nostalgia, particularly that of memories from one's college days.

When we're young we all think that we're unique and believe we experiencing life events for the first time. We all think we're discovering them and forging new paths—even though prior generations felt the same set of emotions, anxieties, and epiphanies.

This turn-of-the-century commencement address reflects the bittersweet evocative emotions experienced by college graduates as they approach their final days of collegiate life and prepare to leave the campus that was once their home, community, source of inspiration, and the basis for their quest for opportunity.[40]

> Some of the paths lead at once into the thick forest, some familiar faces will be seen no more. Some of our paths may be near together for a while, and we can call each other and renew old memories. But the voices will grow fainter and become silent one by one.
>
> White haired college boys sit about us here. We wonder "Did they stand as we and bid farewell to young class-mates?" Will we stand as they so near the end of the journey, and think back over the years to this summer day, when we said farewell and left each other?
>
> Oh, fellows, our lives must be cheery, happy lives. We want to carry sunshine out into the big world. And even at this time we don't want to darken life by sad thoughts. And we know the memories of these old college days will brighten all the way. But it is well that we have this meeting, the last look into each other's faces before we go. We can keep the picture as a final memory of the old boys together.
>
> Boys, we can't stay longer. The moment of parting has come. Good-bye and from heart to heart, as we wait this moment, let there be breathed a silent last good-bye!

(COMPILED BY HARRY CASSELL DAVIS)

It's not only bittersweet but also underscores the powerful legacy shared by all graduates. In fact, it's very likely that your college experience will hold a claim on you long after graduation. Most people can readily recall their first day of arrival on a college campus with its imposing edifices and the hopes and aspirations that came with the opportunity. For many of us, it can still trigger both anxiety and an overwhelming feeling of nostalgia, reflecting a time of change and many firsts, including the first tastes of real independence, personal responsibility, and serious academic challenges. It also means being thrust into a community of peers with diverse backgrounds, triggering all sorts of insecurities and a need for acceptance. It also means experiencing a surge of emotions: a first love, a first breakup, perhaps even a loss of virginity. There are many firsts, all of which can temper our understanding of ourselves. These experiences require us to find ways to contain our emotions, while developing the patience and skill to live in harmony with our peers.

It's an incredible time, with many forces at play that combine to create a forging process where a student's mind is expanded and shaped by exposure to advanced learning, followed by the gaining of perspective and understanding. College, for many, will be the first real taste of independence, newfound freedom, and knowledge, which can be very rewarding, particularly for those with an innate curiosity and an inquisitive mind. Effectively, the experience can put us on a path to adulthood. College is the last experience before entering the next phase, adulthood, taking on all the responsibility that comes with it. It's why, when we look back at those years, we feel an upswell of emotion and nostalgia. The college experience coincides with significant life thresholds, either achieved or experienced, that stand in stark contrast to our lives as adults, which often center on the mundane: finding a mate, creating a family, building ties to your community, taking root, and being mired with responsibility at the expense of freedom and innocence. In fact, becoming an adult, with all its sobering responsibilities, can make you yearn for a simpler time when you first experienced the freedom, excitement, and innocence that came with entering an educational institution for the first time.

Targeting Alumni to Exploit College Connections

Perhaps the best way to exploit one's college connections is by targeting alumni. Most successful alumni want to be helpful to students who went to the same college or university.

An informational interview can add to your perspective and expand your field of vision. Contacting successful alumni and scheduling a dialogue (this can sometimes be done through the Alumni Relations department) to discuss their career moves and achievements can provide invaluable insights. And you can also share with them your interests and goals. Listening to their experiences will help you develop a realistic understanding of business practices and opportunities available post-college. Most executives can identify with what it's like to be in college, so being approached by a humble, willing-to-learn student is hard to deny.

You can't rely on the reputation of a school, its name recognition, or a degree to solve the very real challenges of finding and qualifying for a job in your desired profession. Remember to stay proactive. Stick to the growth mindset and seek help whenever you can. A little outside guidance can help point you in the right direction.

Sure, networking is part of the work environment and membership in an industry or profession, but you have a leg up when you network with your classmates, whether they major in the hard sciences or the arts. Not only will your friend group become more diverse and interesting, but you can start playing career matchmaker with friends from different walks of life. Oh, your college roommate is looking for a job with a high-tech company—it's time to put her in touch with your high school classmate-turned-agent. It can feel just as good to connect your friends with opportunities as it does to make those connections yourself. Start networking with classmates today so that you can pay it forward tomorrow!

Once you graduate and get the job you've been targeting, you'll realize that networking and expanding one's contacts in a variety of occupations and industries can provide invaluable intelligence about job opportunities, career options, and industry changes. It's an invaluable way to increase knowledge, learn from the success of others, get new clients, and tell others about your job, career, and business activities. And the easiest way to expand your network is to build on the relationships with people you know: family, friends, classmates, colleagues, and acquaintances.

Building Social Bridges

The process of networking is not very dissimilar to herding cats. Big egos and different perspectives can be off-putting. Surprisingly, even if you have a falling out with some of your classmates, it doesn't necessarily result in a permanent rift. As time goes by, those years spent in college will ultimately be framed from the perspective of nostalgia, and nostalgia can gloss over a myriad of sins and infractions. For as we age, we become more aware of our mortality, which provides perspective on what's really important as you consider all the implications of your potential options.

Consider the people closest to you. They're bound to be of similar age, and they probably share the same interests, political views, and sensibilities. You listen to similar music, discuss the same movies, and play the same video games. Therefore, you're likely to share the same perspectives and maybe even similar outlooks on life. You find comfort there, even if you aren't stretching yourself.

Then there's the concept of how strangers might be as important to you as close friends and family members. That premise was first brought forth by Melinda Blau and Karen L. Fingerman in their book, *Consequential Strangers: Turning Everyday Encounters into Life-Changing Moments*.[41]

They explain how friendly, casual acquaintances in countless social settings provide a kind of emotional ballast and stability to our lives. Picture the bakery clerk who remembers what kind of pastries we like, the old college buddy who made a critical connection to a business opportunity, or the hospital nurse who offers useful advice and support to patients before and after surgery. Fingerman and Blau contend that these consequential strangers are as vital to our well-being, growth, and day-to-day existence as family and close friends.

The academic underpinnings of the consequential acquaintance concept can be traced back to sociologist Mark Granovetter's 1973 paper "The Strength of Weak Ties."[42] Granovetter argues that job opportunities will most likely come from people in the more distant reaches of your personal network—such as old bosses, former co-workers, and college connections. The phenomenon of social networks has shown that information, resources, and new connections—which are the province of weak ties in all areas of life, not just employment—can have profound consequences on our lives.

How many times have you looked back to your earlier years of high school or a summer job? Do you remember meeting interesting people along the way, but without trying to at least get to know them? Do you regret it? It makes you wonder, what did I miss? Getting out of your comfort zone might be going against the grain for you, but that's what it takes to meet people and expand your network, a concept we will explore in more detail later.

Importance of Feedback

At the edges of your relationships, both personal and work-related, you can garner important information about yourself. How you interact with others and their reaction to you can provide valuable feedback about your individual brand. The process of networking can provide even more insight that can aid in raising self-awareness; people you don't really know are free to react honestly to your introduction and general banter. Networking builds consciousness by allowing you to develop a verbal presentation of your values, beliefs, and professional experiences. Being able to showcase your skills in less than 30 seconds is crucial, not only for forging connections but for building your confidence as a professional.

Accepting Help with Grace

As you build up your network, you'll find that your connections are rooting for you. Typically, they won't mind helping you because they've probably been where you are right now. So if you're looking for career guidance, industry insight, or internship leads, someone in your network can help you out. Most importantly these connections may also play an integral role in helping you secure your first job out of college.

Statistics show that building a strong network creates job opportunities. For example, 35 percent of professionals say they secured their current or most recent job through a professional connection, according to Jobvite's 2018 Job Seeker Nation Study.

On the other side of the coin, 60 percent of survey respondents say they've referred a friend or contact to a company. "Social media, referrals, and word-of-mouth are go-to sources of new opportunities for job seekers," the report states.

Consider the process of qualifying for a job. A hiring manager could easily receive hundreds of two-dimensional applications on a given job opening. From behind a computer screen, how are you, as a recent graduate, going to stand out? Of course, you'll want an attention-grabbing cover letter and top-notch résumé to catch their eye, but a glowing recommendation from a current employee or mutual connection will put you closer to the top.

Don't feel ashamed that someone gave you a hand; *you* still got the job. Listen to anyone map out their career, and at some point, someone in their network probably gave them a bit of a boost, too. What fuels the power of networking is reciprocity. Networking is one of those "I-scratch-your-back-you-scratch-mine" sorts of things, and down the road, you'll probably help someone out too. Sure, it's not *all* about who you know, but you'll find that who you know can really help jumpstart your career.

Contending with the Cycle of Ever-Accelerating Change

In any decade, year, or month, we're always living in a state of flux. It's best to be aware that for any job or business, constancy and longevity aren't guaranteed. This means any worker expecting to make it over the long haul needs to shift from a mindset of permanence (e.g., job security, linear career paths, predictable outcomes) to one of impermanence. Rather than focus inwardly on how you get to the next level on the org chart, you need to look outwardly to understand the nature of change around you. Is it disruptive change? What's shifting in your profession? How is it impacting your industry? Are you honing the right skills and leveraging the best tools to keep pace or get ahead?

Peter Drucker, the educator, author, and management consultant who was credited as the "father of modern management," defined such events as "Crossing the Divide."[43] Every so often there occurs a sharp transformation. Effectively, we cross a divide. In response, within a few short decades, society rearranges itself—including its world view, basic values, social and political structure, arts, and key institutions.

It's only natural that there will be some shifts from creative disruption and the recycling process. But with the right perspective, we can see that it's a necessary adjustment to clean out the system and keep it from becoming calcified and moribund. These moments of disruption generate forces that can override our plans and our future, but there's always another opportunity taking root. Because the market works in cycles, one type of end doesn't have to keep you from adapting. New types of businesses are always emerging, and with your interdisciplinary training, you're welcome to step into those evolving markets.

Not Succumbing to Psychic Entropy

Psychic entropy is a state that leaves us with a greatly reduced ability to deal with complex external tasks or useful inner reflection. We all know what this feels like—being frazzled, fragmented, and unraveled; paralyzed by inertia and self-absorption; worried by thoughts that gnaw at our sense of self-worth and personal value.

Johann Wolfgang von Goethe, in his play *Faust*, is critical of gaining too much knowledge. The main character represents the archetype of the modern man, who is influenced and seduced by Mephistopheles. The good doctor gained knowledge and power, but at the price of introducing disharmony to his soul. Like many scholars, he was drawn to the false promise of a simple life. We're all attracted to the apparent inner harmony of less technologically advanced people, representing the positive side of their limited choices and their skill at handcrafted work. We often fail to see the indiscriminate limitations of human capacity and the loss of individuals failing to live up to their potential. Von Goethe lived in eighteenth century Europe. It was largely an agrarian society with limited opportunity and choice, lived by simple, narrow-minded people who, at best, could only tolerate the slightest of changes.

We are living in a time of a digital revolution. We're on the cusp of witnessing extraordinary technological progress and change. As we use resources, such as coal, oil, natural gas, copper, silicon, and aluminum, to power massive computer farms and process digital information, our technological progress is redistributing Earth's matter from physical atoms to digital information—the fifth state of matter, alongside liquid, solid, gas, and plasma.

Eventually, we'll reach a point of full saturation, a period in our evolution in which digital bits will outnumber atoms on Earth, a world mostly computer simulated and dominated by bytes and code. This staggering accumulation of knowledge will shape future changes. We humans stand at the edge of inheriting a fountain of knowledge that empowers us and diminishes fear.

While we can predict that such changes are coming, it's impossible to know what the changes will be and how they might impact your field of study or your career opportunities moving forward. What is possible, though, is to position yourself to be nimble so you can move quickly with the adjustments. A key part of this positioning is developing and maintaining a strong network that will help you survive disruptive shifts that are the likely result of accelerating change in the world.

Whether it's helping you through hard times, offering you support and companionship, or opening doors for you to new areas of growth or job opportunities, your network of companions will encourage your resilience in the face of reversals, setbacks, and unpredictable change. In a world where change is the only constant, keeping in touch with those who can help you negotiate unexpected turns in the road will become ever more important. The company you keep can make all the difference in helping you survive and even thrive as you traverse an ever-changing landscape.

Don't Walk Alone

Let's briefly return to where we started, in terms of "going it alone"—that is, not going out of our way to make new friends and contacts. It's the way I ended up after graduating from college, and this was well before the technology existed for connected isolation. Going at life solo (or at least in neutral, making no attempt to broaden your relational horizons) is a life of connected isolation, which sounds like an oxymoron, as well it should.

The so-called connected part is that we are linked to the rest of the world through 24/7 social media and other forms of digital communication. The devices and keyboards are at our fingertips. Go online—get on Facebook, Twitter, WhatsApp, or Instagram—and post a comment that can immediately pop up on the news feeds of potentially hundreds or thousands of your friends, and who knows how far it goes from there. Is that the definition of being connected that we should embrace? Will it bring us success and fulfillment? Hardly.

But we have this preoccupation with social media activity. Head down, staring at a screen, we obsessively, relentlessly bang away with our thumbs or other fingers. At such times—for some it's pretty much all the time—we are temporarily (or semi-permanently) oblivious to friends, loved ones, or others who are physically within our reach. Real-world interpersonal relationships are avoided or put on hold. Looking around us, we might see others as disconnected individuals, each without a history or enduring affiliations, and yet there is this connectivity. Some connections are weak; others are more durable. Some are made by belonging to an affinity group; others are related to our jobs and our workplace. Humans need social interaction. We are interdependent social creatures.

Avoiding Social Isolation and Loneliness

As we discussed in an earlier chapter, Henry Thoreau wrote a book about his exploits of living in isolation on Walden Pond.[44] He spent two years living by the pond in a cabin he built. Thoreau claimed that living in isolation provides knowledge of oneself beyond what society could ever teach. In his writing, Thoreau challenges the reader to go back to nature and live the simple life. He contends that one can only discover oneself by removal from society.

But the reality was that Thoreau's cabin was less than a thirty-minute walk from the village of Concord. Revisiting Emerson's Walden Pond lot, Barksdale Maynard writes, "reminds us, first of all, that [Thoreau's] intention was not to inhabit a *wilderness*, but to find *wildness* in a suburban space."[45]

Thoreau was a social creature, Maynard notes, one who lived within view of a well-traveled public road and popular pond, and he had access to a constant stream of visitors. At Harvard, Thoreau was fed a steady diet of classical literature emphasizing lone heroic figures such as Ulysses or Beowulf. We've all been inspired by these stories of heroes who accomplished great feats on their own, but that's not reality. Going it alone in this world seems like an easy path to choose, but it can be a huge burden to bear. That burden is the potential loss of the benefits that come from developing and nurturing relationships outside your close-knit circle. In fact, Thoreau died at just 44 years old in his mother's home, leaving behind a manuscript that no one wanted to publish. It took considerable efforts by the family over many years for it to finally make it into print.

We all have our own unique perspectives. The problem, as we've discussed, is that some of them are simply inaccurate; these hinder our ability to connect with people. Sometimes you just have to work your way through that stuff. Again, it's about leaving your comfort zone. I'll repeat my advice from earlier in this chapter, because it's so critical: Start a conversation (yes, face-to-face) with someone you've seen but not heard. Then try it again with someone else. Turn it into a game, a competition within yourself. Be ready for new opportunities as you grow your circle of connections. Welcome *back* to networking.

Don't beat yourself up over what you've neglected to do. Hindsight is one of life's great teasers—it shows us what we could have done better when we are helpless to go back and change whatever it was. Pledge to yourself that you will work at this. Pursue relationships; if something doesn't work out, move on. Let today be the first day of a better rest of your life.

So, with expectations carefully adjusted, warning hazards noted, and the importance of companionship for your journey understood, you're now ready to start figuring out the specifics of where your particular path will lead you. The next steps begin with plotting your way forward through that all-important decision of choosing the college that's right for you. In the next chapter, we'll discuss the nitty-gritty elements of college selection so you can make the best possible college choice for yourself. I'll also offer some insights from my own life choices for you to consider. Of course, my life is not your life, but we share similar experiences, separated by some decades, of choosing a college that will shape us emotionally, professionally, and academically.

CHAPTER 7

Looking Forward and Planning Next Steps

"The secret of education lies in respecting the pupil. It is not for you to choose what he shall know, what he shall do. It is chosen and foreordained, and he only holds the key to his own secret."

– RALPH WALDO EMERSON

Strategic College Selection

Consider yourself extremely fortunate because you have many options; there are over 4,000 colleges and universities in the United States alone. But with choice comes responsibility. The onus is on you. You can make a frivolous choice or aim for a quality choice. I believe that the quality of our lives is determined by the quality of the choices we make.

Alternatively, if you had been born in Germany or another European country, at somewhere between the ages 10 and 13, you would have taken a national exam to determine if you qualify for higher education. Germany's secondary education (pre-high school level) is separated into two parts, lower and upper. Lower-secondary education in Germany is meant to teach individuals basic general education to prepare students to enter upper-secondary education. The upper secondary level of education funnels students into one of two broad channels, academic or vocational programs. The latter means that attending a college or university is out of the question. German secondary education includes five types of school, but it's only the Gymnasium school that is designed to prepare pupils for higher academic education.[46]

Fortunately, we have choices, but it's up to you, the student, to take the initiative to think strategically, make the right college choice, and gain acceptance into the school. The process involves two parties: the student and the institution that has to decide which students to accept. Surprisingly, both the student and the college have the same goal, and that is the successful graduation of the student.

College offers the student the promise of great potential that can have a lifelong impact. Because of that incredible potential, picking the right school should be a sober, careful, and deliberate decision.

Consequences of Not Doing Your Homework When Selecting a College

Many students feel overwhelmed by the choices available when trying to decide where to spend the next four (or more) years of their lives. It can be tough to decide without getting caught up in the national rankings. *U.S. News & World Report* and other ranking systems are most likely using scoring criteria that aren't truly aligned with your interests, personality, talents, and career goals. The #1-ranked school is not likely to be the best option for you.

In the end, you are the only one who can really choose what college is best for you. You must take ownership of your decision when faced with the rigors and challenges of academic study.

A close look at the college selection experience of Steve Jobs makes this point. We now think of Apple Inc. as a highly successful company and its founder, Steve Jobs, as an icon. But there's an interesting backstory of which many are unaware. Apple's early backers were a "who's who" of venture funds, including Venrock (Rockefeller family), Jock Whitney's fund, Sequoia Capital, and several others. These funds were managed by huge egos who were determined to make Apple a success. The company was a pioneer in the introduction of the personal computer; it struggled for several years to gain acceptance beyond young early adopters. The company almost floundered many times because the audience for its product was too small, but the egos of the fund managers kept the company afloat. Having Steve Jobs as chief spokesperson was useful, given his shared youth and passion for computers. At the time of Apple's founding, he was an immature, uneducated, and petulant fixture of the company, but by the persistent backing of institutional investors, he gained an education that would allow him to successfully proselytize the personal computer to members of his cohort.

Steve Jobs gave a commencement address in which he confessed the following about his decision to go to college:[47]

> At 17, I did go to college. But I naively chose a college that was almost as expensive as Stanford, and all of my

> working-class parents' savings were being spent on my college tuition. After six months, I couldn't see the value in it. I had no idea what I wanted to do with my life and no idea how college was going to help me figure it out. And here I was spending all of the money my parents had saved their entire life. So, I decided to drop out and trust that it would all work out OK. It was pretty scary at the time but looking back it was one of the best decisions I ever made. The minute I dropped out I could stop taking the required classes that didn't interest me and begin dropping in on the ones that looked interesting.

Steve Jobs died prematurely from pancreatic cancer. There is some speculation that he could have avoided premature death by having it properly treated early; he refused treatment for nine months, believing an alternative-medicine diet would be better. It was one of Steve Jobs' most notable regrets, but what may have contributed to his flawed decision-making was his lack of a formal education.

Hobson's Choice

The process of choosing a college, if not properly managed, can turn into a Hobson's Choice—a term derived from an English Tudor businessman, Thomas Hobson. He ran a stable hiring out horses, and he would famously tell his clients, "you can take any horse in the barn as long as it's the horse in the first stall." Effectively, Hobson's Choice was no choice at all, and this is what happened to me.

I grew up in the backwoods of upstate New York, some 70

miles north of New York City. My parents had no money. College to them was pointless; they didn't discourage me, but they were also no help. I didn't have the luxury to swing for the fences in choosing a college. I knew that it was entirely on me to make the selection and gain acceptance. Desperate to get out of my small town, I had to be extremely sensible in my college selection. I had learned from my high school guidance counselor about colleges that offered co-op programs. These programs gave students the opportunity in their junior year to alternate semesters, working one semester followed by classes the next semester. A limited number of colleges had programs that virtually guaranteed a student a job with a company that aligned with their major.

I was aware of only two schools in New York State that offered such programs: Cornell University and Rochester Institute of Technology (RIT). Cornell, an Ivy League university, was prohibitively expensive and extremely competitive, with over-the-top entrance requirements. So I dismissed this option right out of the gate. Alternatively, RIT was a technical college with strong science departments and a brand-new campus supplied with the latest in instrumentation and labs. It also offered cooperative employment opportunities. And assuming the company was based in Rochester, you didn't have to change your off-campus living arrangements from one semester to the next. Two principal employers at that time were Xerox and Kodak.

I also looked at some of the smaller colleges in New England, but they largely offered liberal arts education at prohibitive tuition rates, and I was under the impression that to qualify for a scholarship was equivalent to winning the lottery. So I dismissed those options and ended up with a Hobson's Choice.

I suspect that most high school graduates turn their college selection process into a Hobson's Choice and are often influenced in their selection by some of the shallowest of considerations.

Attrition Rates

There are so many things to consider when deciding which school is the right choice for you: the curriculum, geography, size, cost, student population, public or private, etc. The list of decisions and issues seems to get more complicated every year. It is perhaps no surprise at all that the first-year college attrition rate is almost 30 percent.

Most freshmen head off to college with excitement, high hopes, and rosy expectations, but about one in three won't return for a second year. This number includes those who quit, whether for economic or other reasons, as well as those who have failed out. Colleges and universities are not required to report how many failures contribute to the 29 to 30 percent of college students who leave school during or after their first year. But there's no doubt that college can be tough, particularly for freshmen. Although, as you track the more elite colleges and universities, typical retention rates are above 90 percent.

Why Do Some Colleges Have Such Low Acceptance Rates?

Acceptance rates are an important factor to consider when deciding where to apply. A school's acceptance rate is often considered a measurement of its quality. While this is an accurate perception in many cases, some schools have low acceptance rates for reasons unrelated to the academic achievements of admitted students. Some school administrations have been able to create a marketing mystique about the school disproportionate to its real academic standing.

I would categorize America's 4,000 colleges and universities into four broad groups: public universities, elite private colleges, smaller, lower-tier private colleges, and colleges that focus on very narrow areas of education. Harvey Mudd College, one of The Claremont Colleges, is a good example of the latter. Its education is focused on mathematics, core sciences, and select applied science disciplines. It's a small, elite college with a total enrollment of less than 1,000. Candidates must be passionate about science and score at the top of SAT rankings. Harvey Mudd probably has a less than 5 percent acceptance rate.

A college can have a low acceptance rate for a variety of reasons. The most common reason for a low acceptance rate is a combination of high academic standards and popularity among prospective students. Ivy League schools such as Stanford, Harvard, Yale, Princeton, and MIT have strong name recognition both in the United States and internationally. As a result of their worldwide reputation, these schools command huge numbers of applicants. Consequently, they need to turn away a vast majority of potential students, which also advances their reputations for academic excellence.

Only the most qualified students are admitted, and even those who technically meet their high academic standards might be rejected based on other institutional criteria. In 2019, an impressive 47,498 students applied to Stanford—and only 2,040 were accepted! That's an acceptance rate of just 4.3 percent, giving Stanford one of the lowest acceptance rates in the United States.

Although it's a state university, the University of Virginia has a certain cachet that attracts a lot of applicants. For example, the law school has a sort of unofficial Ivy League standing but at state college tuition rates, which attracts a disproportionate number of applicants, resulting in a very low acceptance rate.

Low acceptance rates also happen at schools that have very specific criteria for admission and are popular for other reasons. Military schools such as West Point and the United States Naval Academy have low acceptance rates because they require applicants to meet other strict criteria besides academic qualifications. Meanwhile, music schools such as Juilliard might have especially low acceptance rates because they're only willing to take extremely talented students in a very specific area of study. Typically, the lower the acceptance rate the higher retention rate.

College Graduation Rate

The goal of a college is to help students obtain a degree, so it makes sense that a high rate of failure or drop-out is a red flag. Some schools are much more successful at graduating students than others, so don't settle for a path that is unlikely to lead to the degree you're paying for.

A college with open admissions, while making school more accessible to all, can mean lower standards and include matriculated students who ultimately decide college isn't for them. About 20 percent of my starting class bailed out in the first year. You can always spot them as they become less animated and more and more removed from academic activity.

A very few students approach college with a firm understanding of their own passion and skills. Their interest and confidence in their major can lead to better academic outcomes. For example, if you have a passion for engineering and math, you are probably going to prefer an engineering school, and so be less mindful of any unrelated shortcomings an institution may have. Many engineers can be introverted, so attending Purdue University with an enrollment of over 30,000 students is probably going to play to their need to be anonymous on a very large, impersonal campus.

But most of us are not in that position. So, we have to rely on our college experience to a far greater degree. We need help in determining our interests, aptitude, and passion and discovering our best career options. We need assistance in making the proper choice so that we're not letting ourselves be pushed into a blind alley or dead end.

Low Student-to-Faculty Ratio

The student-to-faculty ratio is an important figure to consider when looking at colleges. The range of classroom sizes can vary from having a class the size of a conference room to large amphitheater classrooms that can seat several hundred students.

Low student-to-faculty ratios are often ideal, but don't automatically discount a school with a higher ratio. Some universities place large research and publication expectations on their faculty who, in turn, teach fewer courses. Other research universities may devote more time to supervising the research of graduates than undergraduates. As a result, a school can have a very low student-to-faculty ratio, but faculty members may still not have a lot of time for undergraduates.

On the flip side, a high ratio doesn't automatically mean that you'll be neglected by your instructors. If teaching is the top priority at a college, a 20:1 ratio might be better than that 10:1 ratio at a big research-centered institution. No matter where you go, class sizes will vary, along with professor attentiveness. As a rule, state universities are bound to have larger classrooms with high student to instructor ratios, while elite private schools with substantial endowments are more likely to offer a low student-to-faculty ratio. But depending on your major, it's important to keep the student to faculty ratio in proper perspective.

Whatever the school, superior instructors can offer an engaging educational experience. Great professors have the ability to inspire students, take complicated concepts and parse them into understandable components, and offer up insights or keys to understanding.

A college curriculum doesn't need to be trendy or gimmicky to be engaging. As you look at colleges, be sure to spend time exploring their course catalogs. It's important to determine whether a college has a strong first-year curriculum to support your transition into college-level coursework and whether a college offers courses that interest you.

All colleges should have elective courses that make you feel excited, but make sure they have substance and not just fluff. Intriguing classes about pop culture and other mundane subjects are not worth your tuition dollars, since they aren't going to advance your development or transition into a career.

If you think you know what you want to study, look at the requirements for your major at each college. The courses should cover subject areas that attract you and will prepare you well for your desired career or graduate program.

Counseling Services

Does the college you are considering offer comprehensive psychological counseling services, and do they make those services freely available? As an aside, the Center for Collegiate Mental Health has studied the demand for counseling services by students. They have found that the demand for counseling services outpaced growth in enrollment by as much as five times. Probably the last thing on a prospective student's mind is counseling and psychotherapy support, so it's not likely to be on a student's radar as criteria in selecting a college. But I counter from my personal experience that this service is one of the most consequential support services that an educational institution can provide.

I had a moment of personal crisis in my junior year. I was questioning my major and questioning the value of my education. I had this notion or expectation that as part of my education I would discover things about myself, my intrinsic self. To make matters worse, my fellow science classmates were passionate about their studies and, therefore, deeply motivated to take a deep dive into the subject. It was this shared passion that helped to form scientific tribes recruited and led by the faculty of the science department. From my perspective, it was a case of narrowly focused professor "hedgehogs" recruiting like-minded student "hedgehogs."

Although I was attending a third-tier college, the curriculum was intense and demanding. I was drinking from a firehose, and I didn't have the time or the means to focus on my intrinsic self. There is a certain tyranny in being capable enough to keep up but not passionate enough to excel. Years later I came across a quote about an artist who realized that he wasn't good enough to sustain a living. His lament triggered a fellow esteemed artist of his time to say, "better to know the limits of your craft and accept it than to suffer for a lifetime by being a capable artist but knowing that you will never be good enough to be acclaimed by your peers."

Before my college admission, I had met recent graduates who all seemed to emote a composure and confidence that could only come from self-discovery and achievement of greater awareness. In contrast, I felt quite inadequate.

The counselor's response to questioning my selection of major and general anxiety at being lost was to ask me to draw a house. I guess he was setting me up for a sort of Rorschach test, using my drawing to extract the source of my anxiety, while giving him time to subliminally draw me out. I found the whole thing to be a worthless exercise; nothing came of it, and I never returned. I didn't even know enough to ask for a different counselor. I just assumed that they were all the same.

By serendipity, I met someone who had worked at psychological counseling service, and I told her about my experience, along with my disappointment at not gaining meaningful guidance. She suggested personality testing and introduced me to the Myers-Briggs personality test.

I went to the library, and deep into the stacks, I found books on the Briggs-Myers Type Indicator. *It was like an awakening had taken place. This was exactly what I instinctively was searching for.*

From the reference bibliography of the books, I was able to locate articles that offered greater insights into personality types. It led to my discovery of Carl Jung. It was like a magical door was opened to me, which gave definition to my undefined, pressing quest of self-discovery. I needed to know and understand this before it made any sense to select a major.

Psychological Personality Test

Personality tests are designed to identify characteristics of a person's personality. By using personality tests, a clinician can evaluate attitudes, emotions, thoughts, and behavioral traits contributing to one's personality.

In my case, the test was used to aid me in discovering my personality type and inherent personality traits and to provide me with some perspective on the strengths and weaknesses of that personality type, unique individual characteristics or preferences, and prospective career interests. The objective is to allow the student to make informed life choices based on their personality type, traits, and preferences. Also, if someone were to express signs of psychopathology, personality testing can help identify these emotional problems and start the treatment process. Types of psychological personality tests include the following:

- Minnesota Multiphasic Personality Inventory for Adolescents (MMPI-A)
- Millon Pre-Adolescent Clinical Inventory (M-PACI)
- Myers-Briggs Type Indicator (MBTI)

At that time, the Myers-Briggs Type Indicator (MBTI) was most widely used. As mentioned in Chapter 1, it was developed by Katharine Cook Briggs and her daughter, Isabel Briggs Myers. Katharine Briggs was inspired to start researching personality type theory when she first met Isabel's future husband, Clarence Myers. Incidentally, it was shortly after Carl Jung's publication of *Psychological Types* (1921; 1923 in English) that Katharine realized how closely his theories resembled her theories and how much more developed they were. The test is based on an introspective self-reporting questionnaire with the purpose of indicating differing psychological preferences in how people perceive the world around them and make decisions. We all have specific preferences, whether we realize it or not, in the way we construe our experiences, and these preferences underlie our interests, needs, values, and motivation.

According to Carl Jung's theory of psychological types, people can be characterized by their preference of general attitude in four key ways:

- Extraverted (E) vs. Introverted (I)
- Sensing (S) vs. Intuition (N)
- Thinking (T) vs. Feeling (F)
- Judging (J) vs. Perceiving (P)

From these eight MBTI characteristics, there are sixteen possible personality types.

Achievement and Aptitude Tests

Achievement and Aptitude tests measure intellectual functioning and cognitive ability.[48] Achievement tests measure a person's knowledge in a specific area, while aptitude tests assess learning and ability to perform in new situations. Similar to aptitude tests, intelligence tests measure a person's ability to adapt to the environment. Many achievement and ability tests are established standardized assessments with uniform procedures and testing protocols. They can be used in schools, universities, outpatient healthcare settings, and social agencies. Formats include written, verbal, computer-based tests. Examples of this type of test include:

- Wechsler Intelligence Scale for Children (WISC-III)
- Stanford-Binet Intelligence Scale
- Scholastic Aptitude Test (SAT)

Benefits of Psychological Testing

The benefit of psychological testing is that it can alert students to their inherent predilections and aptitude. It brings into clarity and focus, the opportunity to engage with a counselor. You get to check and challenge your own understanding of your personality type and make comparisons to the counselor's feedback from test results and interpretation.

Everyone has different preferences that make up their personality type, and some personalities work better together than others. Your personality type might make it easier to work with one colleague while struggling to collaborate with another.

Our personality types—along with different work ethics, opinions, and approaches—make it difficult to get along perfectly with everyone all the time. However, being aware of your own personality style makes you more likely to observe the traits of those around you. This allows you to adapt your style to theirs or provide them with information in a way that will get their attention, which can go a long way in helping you understand yourself, as well as your colleagues!

The theory behind personality type is that we are born with, live with, and die with our type. It will develop and evolve over time. We might choose to use it differently or apply it differently throughout our experiences. But it will usually remain the same throughout our lives. By understanding your personality type more fully, you can learn to appreciate your strengths and recognize your weaknesses, as well as those of the people around you.

Accepting this about yourself and those around you can improve your ability to work more successfully with colleagues and almost everyone you encounter.

Alternatively, employers use personality test extensively in screening for employees. They are used to making assessments that provide insight into important but intangible information about candidates, such as their personality, values, and work preferences. Armed with this information, human resource managers can gain insight into how well a candidate might fare in any given job.

Hacking the College System

I urge students to hack the college system's psychological support services to gain a deeper understanding of themselves. Most colleges have guidance counselors and psychologists on staff. These services are offered on a passive basis, so if you want to make use of these services, you must be proactive and solicit staff to aid you in your effort of self-discovery. Keep in mind that the first person you meet with may not be the right fit for you. Finding the right counselor to work with is half the battle, and if you don't connect well at your first meeting, don't settle. You're looking for someone who can launch you on the right path for self-discovery. This is a highly personal experience that requires a great deal of tact and understanding and an ability to relate.

The department can provide psychological testing, including personality type testing such as Myers-Briggs and the Big Five. Understanding your personality preferences based on the Myers-Briggs Type Indicator can offer you insights about yourself. It can also serve as an objective basis for comparison to others. An advisor can help you interpret those results to identify your skills and interests. This can facilitate the process of discovering your true skills and aptitude and help you find a connection between aptitude and occupations to find a good fit.

Alternatively, reviewing a list of specific skills necessary for an intended occupation is another approach to finding the right path. This process can guide you as to which occupations are a match to your personal interests and skills. This is a far better way to select a major than basing your decision on a daydream, television show, or a whim of the moment. And it's better than following in the footsteps of a relative without thinking about how it fits with your own preferences and strengths. It's important to know the difference between a fantasy job, a dream job, and a job that offers great quality of life.

Starting the process of identifying your personality type will have major consequences for you in your long-term quest to discover who you really are. For Jung, an early developer of personality typing, it was a lifelong project of self-examination and self-discovery.

I'm advocating the integration of academic study with psychological health counseling. It's advantageous because psychological issues affect academic performance. Many times, the stress of academia will trigger mental health issues. A holistic approach, which includes personality and aptitude testing, can address some of the anxiety students experience. The question is whether the service will be maximized by the student through an introspective dive guided by analysis and objective testing. In my research, most colleges have psychiatrists and counselors on staff. I'm advocating the use of counseling services for self-evaluation purposes, including personality trait testing and aptitude testing. Also, it would improve outcomes if every college made a point to explicitly introduce counselors to students as an intrinsic part of their orientation. Who knows when they may need their services, and given the inherent reluctance of most people to admit to suffering from an episode of poor mental health, shouldn't it be as easy for students to find counselors as it is the student union?

In 2012, 19.9 million students attended colleges and universities in the United States, including 5.8 million enrolled in two-year colleges, 10.3 million in four-year colleges, and 3.8 million in graduate school (census.gov).[49]

For a significant number of these students, their emotional health will be a barrier to academic achievement. According to the Suicide Prevention Resource Center, one-fifth of college students experience a mental illness and increasing numbers of students arrive on campus having received mental health services before starting their college careers.

In 2013, the American College Health Association's National College Health Assessment found that more than half of college students experienced "overwhelming anxiety" at some point during the past year, 32 percent reported feeling "so depressed that it was difficult to function," and 8 percent reported seriously considering suicide.[50]

For me, it was a case of needing self-discovery, analysis, and aptitude awareness rather than self-care psychological counseling. My emphasis on this subject doesn't pertain as much to mental health as it does to evaluate oneself in terms of personality traits, preferences and aptitude. This kind of investigation and analysis can offer insights into self-understanding, and in some cases, prevent mental health crises later.

Students may be fearful about disclosing personal information with a stranger or feel embarrassed if their social circle becomes aware that they're seeing a therapist. I want students to dispel whatever stigma or misgivings they may associate with psychological counseling services. Rather, I advocate embracing it to assist in facilitating self-discovery.

Academic Support Services

Everyone is going to struggle at times with class material. In the first year, you're exposed to a range of essential subjects and courses, and one or more of those subjects may be a challenge for you. My Achilles' heel was writing. High school offered nothing to allow someone like myself to overcome this deficit. This is why looking into a college's academic support services is essential. Whether it's a writing center, individual tutor, or support session that you are looking for, you need to know that this type of help is available. The question is how readily available tutoring support will be when you need it?

Sometimes a tutor can offer up insights that change the course of a student's understanding. Every discipline has components that, if properly explained, can suddenly unleash a newfound comprehension on the part of the student. I have experienced such events many times in various disciplines when suddenly everything seems to coalesce and become foundational in one's understanding of the subject.

In addition to general academic help, realize that all colleges are required to comply with Section 504 of the Americans with Disabilities Act. Qualifying students must be offered reasonable accommodations, such as extended time on exams, separate testing locations, and whatever else may be needed to reduce barriers to their performance. Great colleges include plenty of robust services under and outside of Section 504.

Career Support Services

With over two million college seniors looking to transition into the workforce each spring, it has never been more competitive for graduates to find the right job. Therefore, when evaluating schools, make sure you think ahead to examine what kind of support you can realistically expect from the institution in a successful transition into the workplace four years from now.

Most colleges offer career services, but the question is what kind of resources does the school administration allocate? How large is the staff? What kinds of relationships does the department have with corporations and successful alumni? Do existing corporate relationships offer internships, jobs, and summer employment opportunities?

According to a Gallup-Purdue University study of 30,000 former students who graduated from schools across the county between 2010 and 2016, only 17 percent found their college career centers to be "very helpful" in assisting them with finding jobs.[51]

This is unacceptable. When you consider that the cost of a college education at a four-year private school runs close to $300,000 and that 71 percent of graduates owe an average of

$36,000 in student loans, this makes it essential to prioritize finding meaningful employment after college.[52] The ability of a college to assist in the job search should be a key part of one's school selection criteria.

Does the career services department offer on-campus job fairs, interview preparation, résumé development services, and networking opportunities? Any institution that provides such services is more likely to be supportive of students from the beginning to the end of their careers. Most students attend college with professional aspirations in mind, and a school's career services should be ready and available to help students achieve their goals.

Healthy Alumni Network

We humans are endowed with a tremendous capacity to categorize information and memories. College can have a powerful impact on our development. Given the anxiety and stress of dealing with an onslaught of new information, college can offer a kind of forging process in personal development. But it can also register powerful fond memories that act as the glue that binds your life together with that of your classmates and fellow alumni. It doesn't matter what you did in the past, you can't change it. But you can be nostalgic with your fellow graduates and celebrate the fond memories.

As a student, you're joining members of your cohort to be a part of a community or collegiate environment that will leave a lasting imprint on you, your life, and your career. You and your new cohort will, in some measure, jointly navigate life. Most colleges make an enormous effort to continue their relationship with graduating students by conducting annual homecoming events, class reunions, and other events—often for the ulterior motive of fundraising off their alumni.

Still, to have the ability to immediately link yourself to every person who has ever attended a college upon enrollment is compelling. A school's alumni network can be a powerful tool for providing mentoring, professional guidance, and employment opportunities to its students, even before they graduate.

A business acquaintance graduated from a small elite Philadelphia school, Haverford College. It was originally founded by the Quakers and is now one of the fifteen hardest colleges to get into. The total enrollment is about 1,250 students. He shared with me a Haverford Newsletter, entitled *Economic Endeavors*.

It turned out that this was a newsletter published by Haverford's Economics Department, suggesting that the college produces several newsletters categorized by discipline. In this newsletter, alumni post news about events in their lives. As I was scanning the announcements, I kept seeing a reference to a "White Knight." I asked him what that meant, and without a second thought, he indicated that these were solicitations for investment capital to finance alumni projects. It's amazing that a school founded by humble Quakers, who shunned enterprise and commerce, had progressed into an institution facilitating an investment fund for fellow alumni.

Students should be able to take advantage of their school's alumni network for internships and job opportunities, or there's no point in having one. Typically, alumni at elite schools are eager to volunteer their expertise to students in their field. An active alumni network speaks volumes about the potential for positive outcomes for its students. To have numerous alumni care enough about their alma mater to continue donating their time and money long after graduation says a lot about an institution. You can assume that their college experience was a positive one. This network is a powerful resource that can stack the deck in your favor as you transition into adulthood.

Financial Aid

There are plenty of books and websites available that can provide in-depth financial aid advice. Therefore, I'm going to limit my coverage of this area to several general conclusions that can help guide you.

As a rule, state universities offer far cheaper tuition rates than private colleges, particularly for in-state students. The financial aid that students receive varies greatly between public and private institutions. Private colleges cost considerably more to attend but, as a rule, can offer more financial assistance than public universities. All schools publish the average amount of their aid packages, including the amount that comes from federal grants and loans.

Assuming you qualify as a student, elite colleges can generally patch together grants and loans that will fund somewhere around half of the total cost; it's not likely that your entire tuition will be covered. Smaller elite colleges typically have considerable endowments, which makes them a better source of student aid, with the net effect of bringing your actual cost down to a level that's comparable to in-state tuition at a public university.

When it comes to endowments, there are a number of what I term "pocket battleships" in higher education For example,

Bowdoin College, with a student enrollment of just over 1,900 students, has an endowment of over $2.7 billion, according to their website. There are many other small elite colleges with substantial endowments relative to student enrollment, including Amherst, Swarthmore, and Haverford College to name a few. This allows a college to fund low student to instructor ratios facilitating small, intimate classes.

Good/Better/Best Scenario

It's a reflection of life that, as the Rolling Stones themselves opined, "you can't always get what you want." Perhaps when you feel obstructed, restrained, or disappointed you should think of the setback in a different way—the compromise you must make is also a way of exploring creative choices. As any photographer will tell you, there's never enough light. Every photograph is a compromise between the amount of light you need and the amount of light you have. You must slow down the shutter or open the diaphragm to let more light in, and the way you make that choice is the act of creation itself. Almost every great invention, work of art, manuscript, or sheet of music is borne out of compromise.

Not being accepted into your preferred college is not a catastrophe, rather it's a good, better, or best scenario. One must be philosophical as to which college you ultimately gain acceptance.

There are no right or wrong outcomes. It boils down to a good or better option. But as long as you can make the best of it and take a serious dive into the process of discovering yourself and broadening your understanding of how the world really works, it's an experience that can help sustain you through life.

Of course, every school is different, with different class credit systems and different rules about maximum courses per semester. But no matter where you go to school, navigating life in college is an adjustment that allows for individual growth. You have a lot of required academic coursework and sometimes a required job to help pay for school or earn some extra spending money. Juggling these requirements in a new environment can be challenging.

An acquaintance of mine—a bank executive—has a daughter who was destined to attend Purdue University. She took an advanced college preparatory class while in high school and had to attend a seminar at the Indiana University (IU) campus. The university campus is composed of buildings constructed from Indiana limestone, the same stone used to build most of the capitol buildings in Washington, DC. The rolling hills of southern Indiana, combined with the fall foliage from enormous sycamores, ash, and oak trees can create a magical campus setting and may explain why it was featured in the movie *Breaking Away*.

Based on that one day's experience, she decided to attend IU rather than Purdue. After graduation, she took several administrative jobs, eventually becoming a special assistant to the President of Butler University. This was followed by being named special assistant to the Governor of Indiana. She had an uncanny ability to relate with consequential people, and in such positions, there is zero tolerance for subpar performance and every requirement for competence, unparalleled communication skills, and judgment.

Many of us can't help but ponder what our lives might have been if we had made a different choice, knowing the substantial impact the right college can make. Consider what she might have accomplished had she attended an elite college such as Williams, Amherst, Colgate, Colby, or Bowdoin or any of the elite Northeast schools with enrollments of 3,000 or less. Given her skills, she could have built a network with the titans of industry, the arts, and science. The problem was that she attended a state university with a student body of more than 30,000, which means that she as a student was largely anonymous, with limited ability to network and build relationships.

Creator Mindset

What really counts after four years of education is developing an expanded understanding of yourself, along with a more realistic perspective of the world around you. The other essential component is developing sufficient understanding and confidence to assume responsibility for creating outcomes and experiences in your own life. This realization should trump the notion of waiting passively for other people or a combination of luck and fate to dictate to us. With responsibility comes the obligation to develop the necessary skills to respond wisely to forks in the road. It means taking the initiative to deliberate properly and assess a situation before making choices. But first, we have to be more intentional and investigative in making our first important choice, and that is which college to attend.

Your strategy moving forward can and must be uniquely your own. Nobody can do this for you. As we've said, life isn't a copy and paste of another person's experience, and you can't replicate someone else's story, even if you try. This is your time, your struggle, your journey. That said, it can be valuable to consider how people just ahead of you in life have walked this path. What did they actually encounter, and how did they negotiate the myriad of decisions they faced? What can you take away from their story that might help prepare you for yours? It's in this spirit that I'm sharing my journey in the next chapter.

CHAPTER 8

Looking Back and Mapping the Terrain

"To regret fully is to appreciate how high the stakes are in even the average human life; fully experienced, it turns our eyes, attentive and alert, to a future possibly lived better than our past."

– DAVID WHYTE

History Rhymes

It's important to come to terms with regret. You can't live life without collecting a string of regrets, and I've certainly had my share. One of them is that I didn't have enough information as a young person to make proper decisions when it really mattered, such as which college to attend, what my major should be, or what career trajectory might have been most in line with my skills, interests, and aptitude.

I've had some great opportunities but also many bumps along the way. I decided to write this book because I've often wished that someone had offered me a roadmap, or at least some guidance when I was at the front end of these important decisions in my life. It's in that spirit that I'm offering a brief backward glance to my own story of finding my way through college and career choices, in hopes that you can glean an insight or two that might make the way easier for you than it was for me.

A quote often attributed to Mark Twain is apt here: "History doesn't repeat itself, but it often rhymes." In other words, a person's experience will never be the same as that of someone who precedes them. If history really did replicate itself exactly, you could just copy and paste another person's college and career trajectory and plot your own path accordingly. Of course, that's not how it works because times and circumstances change, and each of us is a unique human being with a singular journey to travel. But the "rhyming" idea offers a useful metaphor. We can learn from other's experiences because, while not the same, history does "rhyme," so that events have enough similarity as to be recognizable, and history can offer some useful lessons. I hope that in looking back at the way I mapped the terrain, you'll find something in your experience that "rhymes" with my history; something that you can hold on to as you go forward.

A Child's View of the World

When I was a child, I had this feeling that my parents were in complete control. They seemed to know everything, from managing the house and dealing with the daily routines to entertaining guests, and they seemed just as adept in their understanding of how the outside world worked. To me, they were omniscient, seamlessly protecting me, providing for me, and making my life both pleasant and entertaining. If there were any problems, I was sure that they could work them out, and if there was something I didn't understand, I knew they could provide the answer, just as they had always explained the many things that I encountered. I was living in my little world of their making. I didn't have to worry about anything. I could go to school, play, have fun, and they would take care of the rest. Effectively, I relied on them, while abdicating all responsibility.

But I remember being disappointed when I was older, perhaps 11 or 12, and I began to realize that my parents weren't as all powerful and knowledgeable as I'd believed. One day I asked my father a question about a school project, and I was surprised when he couldn't help me. It dawned on me that if he couldn't help with a simple pre-high school study assignment, then maybe he wasn't omniscient. As I took notice, I began to realize that my father, in truth, was a very anxious person who constantly worried about even trivial things. He seemed constantly on the defensive, as though he was at risk of being ambushed by the greater outside world at any moment.

I remember watching my father try to do his taxes. He seemed befuddled by the forms, by the nomenclature, by the confusing lexicon. Nor did he have a basic understanding of the theory and mechanics involved in formulating taxable income. He was trying to interpret and resolve the seemingly conflicting statements presented in the directions. Every year, you could feel the anxiety build as April approached. To this day, I do my own taxes. I was determined not to find myself in his predicament. With the time it takes to collect and organize your tax records, you might as well prepare your own return.

At some point, I knew I would have to fend for myself, but I didn't want to live in constant fear, worried and on the defensive. It was paramount that I arm myself. I inferred that with education and knowledge would come confidence; besides, I had this insatiable need to understand how things worked. By that point, I was beginning to feel independent, and I was no longer so much in need of my parents' guidance and protection.

For many people, their early childhood experience represents an ideal to which they long to return (if only from the perspective of nostalgia). How wonderful it would be to continue relying on a powerful parental figure who takes responsibility for our lives, protects us from the world, provides answers to all our questions, and gives solace to our maladies, troubles, sorrows, and hurt feelings!

I inferred, if ever there was a way to attain that scale of knowledge and understanding, it would most likely be found in college. As a teenager, I had only the vaguest notion of how the world worked. From my anxious parents, I had a sense of how complex life can be, but I was innately curious about the mechanics of the way things work. Later in life, I began to appreciate that every professional discipline and practice had its own lexicon and its unique mechanics along with the skills and art and craft needed to excel.

Work versus a Career

Later in life, I witnessed many people living lives of quiet desperation, unhappy in their jobs and unable to extricate themselves from their predicaments. In a way, they had unwittingly placed themselves in a sort of lobster trap of their own making. Just like a real lobster trap, there's an obvious opening, but it's of no use to the enmeshed lobster who is unable to escape. The responsibility of a family, mortgage payments, and the fear of the unknown keeps people from disentangling themselves from the trap of hated jobs, even if there is ostensibly a way out.

It's as if the job they hold came by without their true consent, something that evolved on a random basis due to their inability to define what they really enjoyed doing for a living. They just couldn't muster up the mechanics of defining what it was that they were passionate about and then plotting a game plan to achieve their chosen career.

There is a saying often attributed to Henry David Thoreau: "The mass of men lead lives of quiet desperation." Many people have cited this quote to me, as though they identified with its sentiment, a sort of shared feeling that reflected their own circumstances. In Thoreau's time frame, your father's job was your destiny. The wheelwright who makes wagon wheels and the cooper that made barrels all expected their sons to inherit their trade. People were limited to strict social hierarchies and stations in life. The world was far more structured in that regard, and there wasn't much a person could do about it.

We are no longer bound by these limitations. In modern times, our work options have multiplied. Narrow job expectations determined by birth or class are no longer our destiny; how we earn a living reflects more of our individual qualities and choices, and we are judged accordingly. We are free to choose our profession, providing we have the education, skill, and aptitude to perform. Choosing a career based on superficial facts, rather than a comprehensive review invariably leads to a dead end. We are prone to misunderstand the attractions of certain careers, simply because so much of what a job entails is always edited out of the description, leaving only highlights that are easy to admire. We read of the results, not of the labor required to produce them.

Meaning of Work

We are often seduced by a romantic or glamorous view of prospective jobs, when in fact it entails difficult and tedious labor. We make choices without really weighing the true cost or trade-off that our choices impose. We sometimes pursue occupations that pay well and look good on the surface but require the sacrifice of our own ambition.

A 2013 Gallup poll found that a full 70 percent of workers in the United States are either mildly disengaged or actively disengaged from their work. This means that while most people feel that their roles define them, that definition is one they aren't really that enthused about. Perhaps this is the main reason they aren't engaged or happy with their jobs.[53]

The emphasis on right livelihood is about making sure the goal of living virtuously is not corrupted by our need to earn a living. Consider Freud, who is widely attributed with the quote: "Love and work are the cornerstones of our humanness." This is a paraphrase by Erik H. Erikson. What Freud actually said is that "the compulsion to work" was "created by external necessity." The imperative to work springs from practical demands, not immutable psychic needs.

Bertrand Russell went so far as to claim that "immense harm is caused by the belief that work is virtuous." If we work more than we need to, we deprive ourselves of the time and opportunity for learning, self-development, relationships, and many other things that make for a better world. If we must work, or choose to do so, what matters is that it serves the goal of living well, rather than detracts from it. But David Whyte provides a more thoughtful and balanced perspective on work:[54]

> Work, like marriage, is a place you can lose yourself more easily perhaps than finding yourself. It is a place full of powerful undercurrents, a place to find ourselves, but also, a place to drown, losing all sense of our own voice, our own contribution and conversation. Good work, like a good marriage, needs a dedication to something larger than our own detailed, everyday needs; good work asks for promises to something intuited or imagined that is larger than our present understanding of it. We may not have an arranged ceremony at the altar to ritualize our dedication to work, but many of us can remember a specific moment when we realized we were made for a certain work, a certain career, or a certain future: a moment when we held our hand in a fist and made unspoken vows to what we had just glimpsed. Work is a constant conversation. It is the back-and-forth between what I think is me and what I think is not me; it is the edge between what the world needs of me and what I need of the world. Like the person to whom I am committed in a relationship, it is constantly changing and surprising me by its demands and needs but also by where it leads me, how much it teaches me, and especially, by how much tact, patience, and maturity it demands of me.

Wandering the Wilderness

My biggest fear was that I would graduate from college feeling unprepared and uncertain about my launch into the real world, and that I would fail to develop the confidence to run the gauntlet of finding my first real job. It became increasingly clear that I would likely fail to discover my true aptitude and career passion. Despite my best efforts at exploiting my college's non-academic resources, I failed to find my true career, one that was in harmony with my skills, aptitude, and passion.

As each year went by in college, I became increasingly alarmed by this thought, even as it became progressively clearer to me that my major in chemistry was not in alignment with my goals. Although I had some aptitude, I didn't have the passion or the extraordinary skills to excel in this field of endeavor.

In my last two years of college, I had to make better use of my experience. I threw caution to the wind and started to take a broad array of subjects. When my science guidance professor saw my schedule of courses and the number of unrelated classes, he made critical comments about commitment and serious academic pursuit. Little did I realize that I was expected to show loyalty to the tribe of academic scientists. By taking courses in psychology, investments, and finance, I was showing disloyalty. Later in my career, I would witness the formation of tribes by profession or practice. It always amazes me that people have this tendency to form tribes for any number of reasons, but in so doing they lose sight of the big picture.

I also made further use of non-academic services. I went to the college's career counseling department. I accessed psychological counseling services, where I first became aware of personality testing. But I could never find a connection between personality types and professions.

After qualifying for an academic scholarship, I decided to buy more time by attending graduate school in biochemistry and nutrition. I hoped that by applying myself to a derivation of the field, I could find my niche.

After a year of climbing a high wall and again drinking from a firehose, I started to form some conclusions about my new major. Then one night, I decided to make a radical change in my academic pursuits. I was working late in the lab on a reaction project involving phospholipids, while a more senior graduate student was attending to another lab project. Off on the other side of the lab where our desks were stationed, I could see him holding a model of an organic molecule and talking. No one else was present. Finally, my curiosity got the better of me, and I asked him who he was talking to. He said he was talking to the molecule. He wanted to know how it would respond to a lab reaction.

That's when I realized that molecules and atoms didn't talk to me, and for that matter neither did the universe! I felt totally out of my element. I was tempted to quit right then and there, but I also knew the importance of finishing what you start. The minute you begin to quit when things get tough, you can find yourself spiraling out of control and descending into certain defeat. And once you quit, your threshold for quitting the next time is so much lower. I still had almost a year left to complete my master's degree obligations, and I had to muster all my resolve to finish the program. The future would reveal itself, and ultimately, I found my professional practice and applications in a wide-ranging career of work and accomplishment. So thank God I didn't quit!

As I progressed through graduate school, spending long hours in the lab, I realized that I had this innate need to occupy the high ground and the last place I wanted to be was closeted in a lab, looking inward, and living among the world of atoms and molecules. I needed to be in a place where I could observe and study the horizon and discover the identity of the next wave forming.

I started to wander the wilderness. What I learned was that it's possible to run simulations and review case studies. This was useful in my quest to find meaning and purpose, but I needed to know the true details of how things worked to run realistic simulations. Later it occurred to me that every time you did something new or different it had to be repeated. First you had to organize the parts and mechanics in your mind and run simulations, and only then would you physically perform the task.

This experience reminds me of the Australian aborigines' "walkabout"—their rite of passage for young men in which adolescents undertake a prolonged, challenging journey, sometimes for several months, in search of psychological and spiritual self-definition and maturity. The timing is intentional, since it's during adolescence that the brain establishes and integrates the neural networks in the prefrontal cortex to encode a sense of self-identity, as well as of moral and social conduct. We find that many cultures use rituals at precisely the same stage of development. There's ancient wisdom in allowing time for a metaphorical walkabout in the wilderness so that we may find ourselves.

The Unplanned Plan

After wandering the wilderness of academia and business, I landed a career-defining job completely by serendipity. It started by meeting someone who worked in the investment department of an insurance company. Not long after, I got a job in that same department. I remember my first day as though it was yesterday—a highly charged day of both nervous excitement and sobering responsibility. I was making a dramatic shift in my career. I knew that there was a giant wall of learning that I would have to scale. To catch up with my work colleagues, I was going to have to drink from another firehose, while keeping my wits and sanity about me. The department was staffed largely by Ivy League graduates—and many of them held graduate degrees—for whom this was either their first job or their first serious career position. I can characterize the typical investment specialist as highly intelligent with the ability to absorb tremendous amounts of information, quick on the uptake, and disciplined, with serious purpose in everything they did. Their ability to recall minor details and weave together seemingly disparate facts and figures about corporate credit was, to say the least, astounding.

The office space reflected a consciousness of risk. To an insurance company, risk is present in everything they do. The products sold to clients involved underwriting risk, while the premium income was invested to generate a return for the carrier, which was also subject to risk. The possibility of losing principal was present in both transactions. White colonial trim, brass lanterns, Chippendale furniture, and parquet floors were all a reminder of certain constants in the life of a New England insurance company. And adhering to underwriting investment standards to manage risk in a changing world was sacrosanct. Standards could only be maintained by cultivating discipline. It was drummed into you that the credibility of a financial institution was a non-renewable resource. Once lost, there was no recovering from such an event.

In a world of accelerating change, there was this constant, framed by antique furniture and colonial trim, of a sobering unyielding responsibility. It was a reminder that with change came risk, and it served to emphasize that standards must be maintained. There was an inherent risk with the lowering of standards, and consequently, the staff also had to be held to certain principles. God help you if you showed up with so much as a tattoo!

The department was responsible for investing the life insurance policy owner's premium payments. Those payments went to cover the underwriting cost of the policies and other expenses. The return that was earned on the premium payments went to cover the overhead of the insurance company. There was zero tolerance for any loss of principal, and that knowledge was like a sobering cloud that cast a shadow over the entire office. Risk wasn't some abstract concept; it was a tangible thing we wrestled with every day. I constantly had to ask myself what unconscious assumption I was making that I had no right to make.

One way to manage risk was the use of financing covenants. Borrowers were required to provide financial information, along with certain calculations related to their financial performance and condition. Covenants can offer some protection from credit risk, but they only work if you can get out before the loan reaches insolvency, or before the rest of the credit world has learned the truth about the company's default.

In the Land of the Blind, the One-Eyed Man Is King

My years in the investment department exposed me to a broad range of industries, a number of companies, and many interesting executives that were larger-than-life characters in their time. There were moments when my far-ranging technical exposure gave me perspective and understanding far beyond my age and skill level.

We had an interesting credit opportunity referred to us by a major NYC investment banking firm (now defunct). The company was called OPM, Inc. It specialized in leasing mainframe computers to Fortune 500 firms. This meant financing mainframe computers, which had a depreciable life of 3 to 4 years at best. The leasing business requires exceptional adroitness. The success of the business is based largely on accurately forecasting the residual value of equipment, and those values could fluctuate wildly with business cycles.

The computer hardware industry was dominated by IBM, but it was undergoing enormous changes thanks to brash new upstart companies like DEC, Data General, and Hitachi. Advances in computer chip technology, along with other countries focusing on computer systems, meant the industry was ripe for change.

I had some exposure to computers and software systems. Having attended a technical college, most, if not all, science and engineering majors were required to take computer programming courses. Back then I couldn't see the relevance, but my exposure to programming fueled my interest in computer science and launched a lifetime of reading about computers and solid-state chip advances. I knew the industry was on the threshold of tremendous changes and upgrades to computers in general.

In my reading, I was exposed to Moore's Law, which gets its name from Intel co-founder Gordon Moore. In 1965, he predicted that the number of components in a computer chip would double every year. In 1975, he revised this to every two years. He observed that as computer processing power grew, subsequent components would also get cheaper and undercut the value of existing computers.

This meant that OPM's concentration in computer leasing made their residual values vulnerable to Moore's law and its impact on a computer's residual value. Consequently, I felt uncomfortable funding the company, but as a junior member of an organization, I couldn't turn down the credit based on my personal concerns and limited experience. The company had a history of being funded by several insurance companies, so how could I go against the grain and disparage the company's credit risk. I was desperate to find something that could give me a way to highlight this concern without calling attention to my own convictions.

I decided to do something unconventional. I reached out to our computer department. As a major insurance company, we would routinely purchase several IBM mainframes at a time. Every time IBM came out with a new model it would trigger another round of purchases. I asked to speak to a senior member of the department, who was quite familiar with the company. It turned out that the mainframe computer leasing industry was a small world. I expressed some concern about the company, and he alerted me to a little-known fact that they owned a small Southern bank that had recently been indicted on several counts of check kiting. Bingo, this was a sure sign of liquidity issues, and the likelihood of the company going to elaborate contortions to manage cash flow!

I confronted the investment banking firm that brought us the credit, and they acknowledged knowing about the bank and its problems. However since it was only an indictment and not a conviction, to them it didn't seem worthy to call our attention to this fact.

I don't have to tell you that I turned down the credit. Months later, at a staff meeting, the head of the department—a Yale graduate who relished the ability to criticize subordinates with the benefit of 20/20 hindsight—made an accusatory statement about a computer leasing company that I and another senior officer had endorsed. I said nothing, but the senior officer corrected the department head and recounted the results of our due diligence that had led us to decline the credit.

Many years later, after I had left the company, I remember reading the hefty Sunday edition of the *New York Times*. To my utter amazement, on the front cover of the magazine section was a story about OPM, and the discovery that it was a giant Ponzi scheme. It transpired that a few prestigious New England banks and insurance companies had lost their principal by dealing with OPM and its $225 million fraud. I finally found out what OPM stood for, Other People's Money, an abbreviation that has now passed into the vernacular.

When I look back, I'm convinced that a newly minted economics major from Harvard, Stanford, or Columbia without a broad understanding in other disciplines would have likely funded OPM and thought nothing of it. No one called from the company, my former employer, to thank me for saving their capital and potential embarrassment. To them, I was just doing my job; but to this day, I think about what would have happened had I provided funding to OPM. I would have been subjected to recriminations and ridicule. I would have personally felt guilty about letting down the people who hired me, the recruiters who took a chance on someone who didn't fit the norm.

The Power of Continuous Reinvention

Looking back at my many careers, my broad education proved to be essential in developing a sense of resilience and reinvention as I switched tracks over the years. Don't let anyone steal from you the satisfaction of resilience, deliverance, and vindication of your skills and heart.

Nature doesn't distribute all its gifts to any single individual. In college, you may know a classmate that is brilliant in math but couldn't compose an essay to save his or her life.

You can meet someone who is a gifted writer but has an irrational fear of spiders. Your gifts are yours alone but discovering and applying them in the absence of clear direction is a challenge.

While I worked at the insurance company, we hired a graduate of Columbia University's MBA program. As we were chatting, a helicopter was landing on a high rise down the street from our building. As we watched it descend, the new hire curiously asked whether a small plane could land on the helipad. It was then that I realized the difference between academic smarts and common sense—and a very basic understanding of the laws of physics. You can't assume that both are inherently tied together.

A Zen Story

Sometimes, no matter how much we plan and plot, our work life takes us in unexpected directions. Surprisingly, we sometimes end up coming right back to where we started! Let me share a story that makes this very point:[55]

> There was once a stonecutter who was dissatisfied with himself and his position in life. One day he passed a wealthy merchant's house. Through the open gateway, he saw many fine possessions and important visitors. "How powerful that merchant must be!" thought the stonecutter. He became intensely envious and wished that he could be like the merchant.
>
> To his great surprise, he suddenly became the merchant, enjoying more luxuries and power than he had ever imagined, but he was envied and detested by those less wealthy than himself. Soon a high official passed by, carried in a sedan chair, accompanied by attendants, and escorted by soldiers beating gongs. Everyone, no matter how wealthy, had to bow low before the procession. "How powerful that official is!" he thought. "I wish that I could be a high official!"
>
> Then he became the high official, carried everywhere in his embroidered sedan chair, feared and hated by people all around. It was a hot summer day, so the official felt very uncomfortable in the sticky sedan chair. He looked up at the sun. It shone proudly in the sky, unaffected by his presence. "How powerful the sun is!" he thought. "I wish that I could be the sun!"
>
> Then he became the sun, shining fiercely down on everyone, scorching the fields, cursed by the farmers and

laborers. But a huge black cloud moved between him and the earth, so that his light could no longer shine on everything below. "How powerful that storm cloud is!" he thought. "I wish that I could be a cloud!"

Then he became the cloud, flooding the fields and villages, shouted at by everyone. But soon he found that he was being pushed away by some great force and realized that it was the wind. "How powerful it is!" he thought. "I wish that I could be the wind!"

So, he became the wind, blowing tiles off the roofs of houses, uprooting trees, feared and hated by all below him. But after a while, he ran up against something that would not move, no matter how forcefully he blew against it—a huge, towering rock. "How powerful that rock is!" he thought. "I wish that I could be that rock!"

Then he became the rock, more powerful than anything else on earth. As he stood there, he heard the sound of a hammer pounding a chisel into the hard surface and felt himself being changed. "What could be more powerful than I, the rock?" he thought.

He looked down and far below him, he saw the figure of a stone cutter.

This parable demonstrates the endurance of truth. There are certain truths that transcend time and the decay of civilizations. This story is a reminder: at the end of your quest or sojourn, you may find yourself at the place where you started. The path of self-discovery is not always linear and can, like God and shopping carts, move in mysterious ways. You have unique skills and your purpose is to discover what they are and find the appropriate place to practice them.

To make the right decision requires perspective. The Zen story is all about the protagonist in the story expanding his perspective, which allows him to gain the wisdom to accept his station in life.

Work will be an important guiding force of your life, no matter what you decide to do. It can make or break you, and you may find that, like the stonecutter, you sometimes come full circle rather than always forging straight ahead.

Conclusion: Finding Your Way

CARL JUNG SAID, "THE ACHIEVEMENT of personality means nothing less than the best possible development of all that lies in a particular, single being. . . . Personality is an act of the greatest courage in the face of life and means unconditional affirmation of all that constitutes the individual, the most successful adaptation to the universal conditions of human existence, with the greatest possible freedom of person."

This is exactly what I wish for you, as you use the college experience to discover your personality traits, strengths, and aptitudes. This, combined with your newfound knowledge, will allow you to venture thoughtfully into the amazing journey that lies before you.

It takes courage and a great degree of self-knowledge to step onto an uncertain path and navigate the many possibilities that are yours alone to explore.

It's important to adjust one's expectations about what college can deliver. It's best to be bold and exploit all the opportunities offered in academia. When you do falter, may you learn from adversity with both humility and the determination to continue to grow. I also hope you will find the courage to reach out to trustworthy individuals in your college cohort and beyond, so that you can surround yourself with those who will be treading a similar path. Better yet, if you can assemble an ever expanding band of benevolent fellow travelers, you will have achieved something every bit as meaningful as your diploma.

College attendance, as well as life, isn't about winning awards and/or diplomas. After the rush of achieving one's goal or experiencing a win, nothing has really changed. You still are you and that makes the winning of awards or gaining a diploma rather esoteric. They are all rather meaningless unless they have had a meaningful impact on the recipient. Typically, lasting understanding can only be achieved by a gain in perspective. Then and only then have we achieved a legacy of discovery and renewal.

The reality is that we don't have any real appreciation for the risks and consequences in life. One of those risks is that our lives become something else: an odd assemblage of habits, objects, and impulses, and not even a story at all.

It's amazing how the right set of words at the right time, as experienced by Carl Jung, can lead to an understanding and a substantial advancement of one's perspective and discovery! College offers the opportunity to advance one's understanding and perspective but only you will know if that diploma earned delivered on that promise.

Attending college should never be just about gaining a diploma and winning awards. While a diploma may display latent promise, a keen interest in a field of endeavor, and perhaps some aptitude, it does not necessarily translate to professional ability. The good news is that there's a host of other factors that do. This brings me to the second reason that a certificate, diploma, or award should not be the sole focus of your time at college; they are inanimate things that end up sitting on a desk or hanging on a wall collecting dust. For a diploma to be meaningful, it should signify a personal progression toward achieving greater understanding and lasting impact through a gain in perspective. Then and only then are you positioned to potentially set out on a journey of lifelong self-discovery and renewal.

The Heisenberg Uncertainty Principle, from the study of quantum mechanics, deals with the structure of atoms (combinations of protons and electrons). It says the act of measuring an electron of an atom causes it to move. Consequently, the position and velocity of a molecular object cannot both be measured exactly at the same time. Developing an understanding of yourself can impact the way you perceive the world, and it can change your perspective. The act of advancing one's perspective will likely result in that person no longer being quite the same. Alternatively, the quest for understanding and self-discovery doesn't happen overnight; it takes a long time to identify and connect all the dots. The process is closer to that of a pilgrimage.

By taking stock of your values, interests, personality characteristics, and skill sets, you may avoid the risk of finding yourself adrift; your life becomes something other than an assemblage of habits, objects, and impulses. Rather it becomes a coherent story with a narrative of your own making.

The alternative can best be summarized by what I said earlier in the book: most of us may well find ourselves disappointed, moving from one scene to the next without purpose as we wandered from high school to college, then to our first job.

It's amazing how the right set of words at the right time can lead to an understanding and a substantial advancement of one's perspective and self-discovery! College offers you the opportunity to advance your understanding and perspective, but only you will know if that diploma, once earned, delivered on that promise.

Hopefully, this book will facilitate your road to self-discovery!

Epilogue

I selected the words of poet Robert Frost to begin Part I of this book because his life story and his most famous poem, "The Road Not Taken," can serve as an allegory for what most students have to confront as they progress through higher education.

College students are expected to discover their true talent and interest and select a major. Then, they must establish basic proficiency in that subject or discipline and sell that talent to the world that awaits them after graduation.

As an American poet, Frost depicted realistic scenes of New England life familiar to the common man. His famous works include "Fire and Ice;" "Birches;" "Out, Out—;" "Nothing Gold Can Stay;" and "Home Burial." "The Road Not Taken" is often read at graduation ceremonies across the United States to illustrate the choices they must make. As a special guest at President John F. Kennedy's inauguration, Frost achieved the zenith of his poetic career to become the unofficial "poet laureate" of the country.

Frost's personal story is just as inspiring. He experienced many setbacks and tragedies that could have destroyed an ordinary man. He had extraordinary talent, but his life was based on a set of contradictions. Unlike many of his predecessors, he never completed college—and yet he became a professor of English at Amherst College. While his peers were content to roam the halls of academia, he relished working with his hands and embraced hard labor, spending twelve years as a New England farmer. His experience with stone walls is self-evident. As a New Hampshire farmer, no matter where you set your plow, you're going to run into granite rock and boulders. They call it the granite state for a reason. Those romantic stone walls that he wrote so eloquently about in his poem "Mending Wall" are strewn across the New England countryside for a purpose, and they typically aren't there to corral animals. Rather, they serve as a repository for all those stones running afoul a farmer's plow.

Frost's public image has also undergone many transformations. Initially, he was viewed as a wise and genial man. In his lifetime, he earned four Pulitzer Prizes and twenty honorary doctorate degrees from many prestigious universities. Possibly in an attempt to admonish his own true nature, he projected the image of a mild-mannered, gentlemanly academic. Later, he went on to be perceived as the farmer poet offering homespun wisdom, but as time progressed, he was perceived as a selfish, egomaniacal, cruel, petty, and angry man. His marriage deteriorated to such an extent that his wife declined to summon him to her deathbed. It's a strange tale for a poet with the gift of superlative poetry who couldn't even summon the words to romance and inspire his own wife. Lawrence Thompson, a close associate of Frost, published an extensive biography a decade after Frost died. He had grown to despise Frost and used the biography to exact his revenge.

I shudder to think what might have happened to Frost if he had been a mere mortal like us, without all those gifts and talent. The problem with having talent is that it can often color the reality of its host. Given our personal biases and tendency to overestimate our skills, even a little talent can turn our heads. Talent is something we inherit, but we can't measure its quality and durability. Only the world at large can make that assessment. Talent can often become an obsession since it's the gateway to sought-after fame and fortune. It's better to know the limits of one's talent than to be deceived and give 100 percent of one's efforts to strive for fame and fortune at great sacrifice to ourselves and those around us, only to end in failure. Frost could have easily gone from being a subsistence farmer to a subsistence poet. Talent makes great demands upon its host. His love for poetry was an affliction for him. He didn't have a choice but to cast his fortune as a poet. Frost said it best: "To be a poet is a condition, not a profession." However, he was one of the fortunate ones; he knew what he wanted to be, and he had the talent and constitution to back it up.

Originally, he enrolled at Dartmouth College but left early. Later, he attended Harvard University for two years but again failed to earn a degree. Instead, he got married and moved with his wife, Elinor, and children to a farm in New Hampshire—property that Frost's grandfather had purchased for them—and attempted to make a life as a farmer but endured a hardscrabble life.

Until he achieved literary success, he was financially dependent upon his grandfather, moving his family around endlessly at various attempts at farming. He sought to subsidize the family's existence by taking teaching positions. Before publishing his bestselling poetry volumes, he had already earned a reputation in education circles as a teacher and lecturer. In between farming and raising a family, he taught part-time at nearby Pinkerton Academy to share his love of literature and to earn some hard cash to subsidy his subsistence farming. In fact, throughout most of his life, he was associated with a university, either as guest artist, lecturer, or instructor—despite never having earned a degree.

Although his farming endeavors never worked out, it was a fruitful time for Frost's writing. Frost acclimated himself to a rural life which became a source of inspiration for his writing. He used the time at his remote New Hampshire farm to ruminate and write. Living in New Hampshire with no radio or TV and no shopping malls, his mind was free to dwell on one thing—making the most of his talents as an observer and poet to complete his first body of work. He had a unique connection with the land, and he was able to depict it from a fresh perspective, as reflected in the quote "a poem begins with delight and ends in wisdom." After reading his poem about stone walls or the mere mention of a woodpile, you never quite view them the same. Having worked as a hired hand on a farm, to this day a stone wall in disrepair or a mangled woodpile have a claim on me.

He must have known what poet Mary Oliver (1935–2019) knew—if the poem was thin, it's because the poet hasn't fully studied his subject. "The poet must not only write the poem but must scrutinize the world intensely, or anyway that part of the world he or she has taken for subject," wrote Oliver. "If the poem is thin, it is likely so not because the poet does not know enough words but because he or she has not stood long enough among the flowers—has not seen them in any fresh, exciting, and valid way." Her poem "The Journey" offers some respite to Frost's behavior, even though it was composed and written without thought or consideration of him.

But it was also a difficult period in his personal life. He experienced the death of two of his young children, followed by Marjorie, the third of his six children. Four years later, his wife died. Decades later, death would follow him, with the suicide of his son followed by the death of a daughter who died in childbirth.

Men with great talent can unintentionally inflict pain on their offspring, particularly on their sons. Sons admire their fathers, and they are born with an insatiable need for approval and validation from them. The problem exists when a father in possession of great talent makes it an impossible task for a son to follow in his footsteps. Just as Icarus flew too high with inferior wings, sons are destined to feel like failures in comparison to the achievements of a great man. Frost's eldest son, who also took up poetry, killed himself with his hunting rifle. His body was discovered in their stone farmhouse. Frost found reasons to blame himself for every one of these tragedies, although the family and others attributed the son's suicide to a strain of mental illness that haunted the family. His two living children, Irma and Lesley, ultimately sought protective distance from him and the maelstrom that had swept over the family.

Frost spent his first forty years as an unknown subsistence farmer. He was a late bloomer, but somehow he mustered the courage to sell his farm and dedicate his life to poetry. He exploded on the scene after returning from a trip to England. It must have taken considerable courage to throw caution to the wind and expose himself to public scrutiny and his life's work to critics. He left his farm, where he labored anonymously alone with his family, and put himself on a public stage exposed to public and literary review. A person's need for recognition and admiration is strong, even for an introvert like him. Talent craves that moment in the sun, but can it withstand the sun's glare and scrutiny? He went from farmer to full-time crafter of poetry and public entertainer. Poetry is not just wordplay. It offers unique insights and perspectives—sometimes a new way at looking at things, emotion, and adversity.

I admire his resourcefulness as a tactician. He instinctively knew when and how to change the course and direction of his life. He knew he had to be an evangelist promoting his poetry and his unique perspective on life. He did this in full measure, selling the farm and embracing a world of arts and letters. He went from living an anonymous life as an introvert to being a self-promoter. We envy those people with talent, but we fail to recognize that talent comes with an enormous appetite. It demands attention and views everything else family, friends, and obligations as a distraction. It's selfish to the core. We surrender to our talent to the point of being afflicted. He referred to his own poetic ambition as a condition.

People are complex, and life takes its toll. But his interpretation of nature and everyday life more than compensates for his personal failings. Winter in New Hampshire is rough. I have spent several winters there, and I know how harsh and intensely cold it can be. In winter, the soil becomes as hard as concrete. To be a farmer under such circumstances is a cruel and harsh experience. There's a coarseness to farming. It means battling nature and the weather. Nature can be a harsh advisor, causing many farmers to become coarse and insensitive. In spite of this, Frost was never robbed of his own unique affirmative poetic view of the world. Instead, it toughened him and gave him the resilience to persevere. As the years caught up with him, he developed a sense of humility, as expressed by this quote: "I am a writer of books in retrospect. I talk in order to understand; I teach in order to learn."

People typically present to the outside world their best, most civilized persona. I am not surprised that Frost was a complex individual. He paid a heavy price for his talent. It took a toll on his life and family, but his poetry captured the essence of what he pondered. He changed the way we perceive ordinary events and things found in nature, unlike anyone before and after him. He was a one-in-a-million talent!

When we come in contact with great men, we see the glory of their great work. We fail to see the devastation that they leave behind in their personal life. Frost referred to being a poet as a condition or as an affliction, out of his control. Talented people typically suffer from two afflictions. They usually are also unabashed romantics. I define a romantic as person who writes checks that they can't possibly cash.

Typically, their behavior is usually at the expense of those around them. For example, Frost had an affair with a neighbor's wife immediately after the death of his wife. Four of his six children died prematurely, but one can't help but wonder what would have happened had he provided the resources and care for their protection. It's these great, talented romantics that typically in their speeches before college graduates echo the typical advice, "follow your passion"—usually dispensed without any provisions, whether it's at the expense of common sense or even in the face of mediocrity.

The reality is it takes a sober self-examination and considerable testing and deliberation to know which fork in the road to take. The cues are there to be found, provided you are willing to flush them out, carefully dissect them, and objectively make an evaluation, weighing one's options.

Acknowledgments

WHEN ROBERT PIRSIG'S *Zen and the Art of Motorcycle Maintenance* was first published in 1974, it attracted a lot of attention. In fact, it caught my attention. I was in graduate school at the time, questioning not only my choice of major but also my competence. I was lost, unsure of my direction and purpose in life. At the heart of the matter was that I didn't understand myself, nor did I know or appreciate my personal skills or aptitude; I was able to get by academically but not talented enough to really excel.

I was the first in my family to attend college. Given my family's limited resources, it took a lot of planning and maneuvering to fund my education. I was fortunate to go on to graduate school on a full ride, but I felt awful about taking this money and not meeting expectations.

The premise of Pirsig's book centers on his motorcycle journey from Minnesota to California with his son and motorcycle companions, a husband and wife. Along the way, he ruminates and pontificates. Slowly we discover that he had undergone a personal crisis of his own in academia, which I could relate to.

What I found so compelling about the book was its emphasis on the mysticism, Zen, and Eastern and Western philosophies. It dealt in the metaphysical and theoretical realm, providing indirect, lateral perspective. There were no straight lines in his musings. He illuminated for me the indistinct parts of life; its shadows and asymmetrical nature. Just as there is dark, unseen matter in the universe, so there is the presence of intangible parts of life that are just as relevant as matter itself. As a science major, this was all new to me.

He acknowledges wrestling with his own personal demons. He refers to his prior self, before his mental breakdown, as Phaedrus after the character in Plato's dialogues. Philosophy, especially metaphysical philosophy, makes claims that cannot be verified by everyday experience or by the scientific method; after all, the human mind is complicated, and it craves meaning.

The trip was punctuated by his endless musings on a variety of subjects, including the petty. I remember distinctly how Pirsig took umbrage at his companion's BMW motorcycle. His criticism seemed to emanate more from jealousy than principle. Effectively, he made himself vulnerable and human in his everyday musings.

But even more compelling were the insights and advances in perspective offered by his book which gave acknowledgement to those indistinct parts of life. My book can open a gate or portal to self-understanding, reflection and reconcile, but, just as important, it will also advance the reader's perspective and empower them in their navigation of a college education.

Endnotes

Preface

1 Selingo, Jeffrey J., "Two-Thirds of College Grads Struggle to Launch Their Careers," *Harvard Business Review,* May 31, 2016.

2 Chambliss, Daniel F., and Christopher G. Takacs, *How College Works* (Boston: Harvard University Press, 2014).

Chapter 1

3 Kaag, John, and Martin, Clancy, "At Walden, Thoreau Wasn't Really Alone With Nature," *New York Times,* June 10, 2007.

4 Sullivan, Walter, "Einstein Revealed as Brilliant in Youth," *New York Times,* Feb. 14, 1984. https://www.nytimes.com/1984/02/14/science/einstein-revealed-as-brilliant-in-youth.html.

5 Ravin, James G., "Albert Einstein and his mentor Max Talmey," *Documenta Ophthalmologica,* p. 1-17, March 1997.

6 Freeman, John, BBC Film interview of Carl Jung, 1957, 14 minutes and 11 seconds into interview.

7 Jung, Carl, *Collected Works of C.G. Jung, Volume 6: Psychological Types* (Princeton: Princeton University Press, 2014 e-book; originally published in 1923).

8 Owens, Molly, "The History of Katherine Briggs, Isabel Myers, and the MBTI," Truity, June 30, 2012.

Chapter 2

9 Plummer, Brad, "Only 27 percent of college grads have a job related to their major," *Washington Post,* May 20, 2013.

10 Liebenberg, Jené, "Story of the Day: Four College Students Were Out Partying Late at Night," Amo Mama, June 4, 2021. https://news.amomama.com/264546-story-day-four-college-students-were-out.html.

11 Delbanco, Andrew, *College* (Princeton: Princeton University Press—Bowen Series, 2012).

12 Chen, James, "Commerce: What It Is, How It Differs from Business and Trade," Investopedia, August 14, 2022.

13 "Zero Sum Game (and Non Zero Sum)," WallStreetOasis.Com, 2021.

14 Dweck, Carol S., *Mindset* (New York: Random House, 2006).

15 Covey, Stephen R., *The 7 Habits of Highly Effective People* (New York: Free Press, 1989).

Chapter 3

16 Hanson, Victor Davis, "The Deflation of the Academic Brand," *National Review,* August 14, 2018. https://www.nationalreview.com/2018/08/academic-brand-deflated-elite-degrees-worth-less/.

17 Slaughter, Brittany, "Nearly 40 percent of graduating college seniors feel unprepared for a career: survey," The College Fix, May 9, 2019.

18 Menand, Louis, "Everybody's an Expert," *New Yorker,* November 27, 2005.

19 Menand, Louis, "The De Man Case," *New Yorker,* March 17, 2014.

20 Dunning, Brian, "Mystery of Dyatlov Pass," *Skeptoid Podcast* 108, July 8, 2008.

21 Andrew, Robin George, "Has Science Solved One of History's Greatest Adventure Mysteries?" *National Geographic,* January 28, 2021.

Chapter 4

22 Livingston, Sterling J., "Myth of the Well-Educated Manager," *Harvard Business Review,* January 1971.

23 Jennings, Eugene E., *Routes to the Executive Suite* (New York: McGraw Hill, 1971).

24 Hesse, Hermann, *Beneath the Wheel* (New York: Bantam Books reissue, 1976; originally published in 1906).

25 Gray, Peter, "How Schools Thwart Passions," *Psychology Today*, November 25, 2018.
26 Jacobs, Peter, "Professors Reveal The Craziest Things Students Have Done During Class," *Business Insider*, October 11, 2014.
27 Kulich, Steve J., "Going Through Waves of Cultural Adaptation," Shanghai International Studies University, 2015.
28 Deighan, Katherine, "A Reflection on My First-Year Experience," DePauw University website, May 12, 2016.
29 Dibdin, Emma, "Are You Too Judgmental? How to Limit Fundamental Attribution Error," PsychCentral, November 9, 2021.

Chapter 5

30 Conrad, Peter, "William Golding: The Man Who Wrote Lord of the Flies by John Carey," *Guardian*, August 29, 2009.
31 Bregman, Rutger, "The Real Lord of the Flies: what happened when six boys were shipwrecked for 15 months," *Guardian*, May 9, 2020.
32 "Generations," Wikipedia; Jaeger, Hans, "Generations in History: Reflections on a Controversial Concept," *History and Theory*, 1985.
33 "Millennials: Confident. Connected. Open to Change." Pew Research, February 24, 2010.

34 Micu, Alexander, "Only about half your friends actually consider you a friend," ZME Science, Jan. 31, 2018.; "Friendship Reciprocity and Behavioral Change," Massachusetts Institute of Technology, August 2016.

35 Schwab, Klaus, "The Fourth Industrial Revolution: what it means, how to respond," World Economic Forum, January 14, 2016.

36 Jobs, Steve, "You've got to find what you love," Stanford News, June 12, 2005.

37 Sciutto, Jim, "Life aboard a U.S. submarine," CNN, October 26, 2017.

Chapter 6

38 Massie, Siegrid, "It's not what you know, it's who you know," *Baylor Lariat*, September 1, 2021.

39 Brooks, David, "The Blindness of Social Wealth," *New York Times*, April, 16, 2018.

40 Davis, Harry Cassell, *Commencement Parts* (New York: Hinds, Noble & Eldredge, 1898).

41 Blau, Melanda, and Fingerman, Karen L., *Consequential Strangers* (New York: W.W. Norton, 2009).

42 Granovetter, Mark S., "The Strength of Weak Ties," *American Journal of Sociology*, May 1973.

43 Drucker, Peter F., *The Daily Drucker* (New York: HarperCollins, 2004).

44 Heitman, Danny, "Not Exactly a Hermit: Henry David Thoreau," *Humanities*, September/October 2012.

45 Maynard, Barksdale W., "Earth's Eye," Introduction Essay, *Walden Pond*, Concordlibrary.org, 2004.

Chapter 7

46 "German Education System," Study in Germany, 2020.

47 Jobs, "You've got to find what you love"

48 Cherry, Kendra, "What Are Aptitude Tests?" verywell-mind, September 16, 2022.

49 Census figures; "Best Practices for Mental Health Services in Colleges and Universities," Oklahoma State website, https://www.okhighered.org/campus-safety/resources/CBP-mental-best-practices-higher-ed.pdf.

50 American College Health Association's National College Health Assessment Survey, Spring 2013.

51 "Gallup and Purdue Reveal Findings on U.S. College Graduates' Well-Being," Gallup, May 6, 2014.

52 Sherman, Michael, "How to Evaluate College Career Services," Bright Horizons: College Coach, August 11, 2017.

Chapter 8

53 Blacksmith, Nikki, and Harter, Jim, "Majority of American Workers Not Engaged in Their Jobs," Gallup, October, 28, 2011.

54 Whyte, David, *Crossing the Unknown Sea* (New York: Riverhead Books, 2001).

55 Ambler, Charlie, "Zen Story: The Stonecutter," Daily Zen, May 6, 2015.

Index

A

B

C

D

I

J

K

L

M

N

O

P

T

U

V

W

X

Y

Z

About the Author

PETER KLEIN is the principal and owner of Secor Advisors Group, a financial services company that delivers high-level advice and market support to top firms. He was born in Austria in a refugee camp, and his journey triggered a lifelong inquiry into the human condition. He has spent a lifetime connecting the dots across many disciplines, including science, social science, economics, and medicine, in what appears to be an asymmetrical world. He holds an MBA and a graduate degree in biochemistry and nutrition and lives in Indiana.